BARKING BRILLIANT

A KIDS GUIDE TO DOGS

BRIAN THOMAS

Copyright © 2024 by Brian Thomas

All rights reserved.

No part of this book may be reproduced in any form or by any electronic or mechanical means, including information storage and retrieval systems, without written permission from the author, except for the use of brief quotations in a book review.

INTRODUCTION

Dogs are more than just animals; they're companions, helpers, and even heroes. Have you ever wondered why dogs seem to understand us in ways no other animal does? There's something truly special about the bond between humans and dogs, a connection that stretches back thousands of years. But what exactly makes them so extraordinary?

Let's start with their ability to connect with people. Dogs have a way of looking at you with those big, soulful eyes, as if they're trying to read your mind. And guess what? They kind of are! Over centuries of living alongside humans, dogs have developed an incredible skill: they can read our emotions. Scientists have discovered that dogs can pick up on facial expressions, tone of voice, and even our body language. If you're sad, your dog might snuggle up close. If you're happy, they'll wag their tail and bounce around, sharing your joy. It's like they're emotional mirrors, always reflecting what you feel.

But their superpowers don't stop there. Dogs have some of the best senses in the animal kingdom. Take their noses, for example. A dog's sense of smell is so powerful that they can sniff out things we'd never notice. Have you ever seen a dog sniffing around the park? They're not just smelling dirt—they're picking up a whole world of scents, from the footprints of other animals to the faintest whiff of your picnic sandwich. Some dogs are trained to use their noses to save lives. Rescue dogs can find people trapped after an earthquake, while others can detect illnesses like cancer just by smelling someone's breath. That's right—dogs are like living, breathing superheroes.

Then there's their loyalty. Dogs stick by their humans through thick and thin, no matter what. Think about Balto, the sled dog who helped deliver life-saving medicine to a small Alaskan town during a deadly outbreak, or Hachiko, the dog in Japan who waited at a train station every day for years for his owner to come home, even after the man had passed away. These stories aren't just tales—they show how deeply dogs care for their people. And it's not just famous dogs; even the furry friend in your backyard feels a strong sense of loyalty to their family. It's why dogs are often called "man's best friend," a title they've earned over and over.

Another thing that makes dogs special is their incredible diversity. Think about it: there are over 340 recognized breeds of dogs around the world, each with its own unique look and personality. From tiny Chihuahuas to massive Great Danes, every breed is special in its own way. Some were bred for specific jobs, like herding sheep or pulling sleds. Others were bred simply to be great companions. Each breed tells a story about the people and cultures that shaped it. Even mixed-breed dogs, those lovable mutts, carry a mix of traits and histories that make them one of a kind.

Dogs also have amazing physical abilities. They can run fast, jump high, and swim like pros. Greyhounds, for example, can reach speeds of up to 45 miles per hour, making them one of the fastest animals on land. Border Collies are famous for their intelligence and agility, often seen zig-zagging through obstacle courses with lightning speed. And let's not forget water-loving breeds like Labrador Retrievers, who can dive into a lake and retrieve a stick with ease.

Whether they're sprinting, leaping, or paddling, dogs are built for action.

But dogs aren't just about brawn—they've got brains too. Some dogs are so smart they can learn hundreds of words, solve puzzles, and even perform complex tasks. Service dogs, for example, are trained to help people with disabilities. They can open doors, pick up objects, and guide their owners safely across busy streets. Therapy dogs bring comfort to people in hospitals and nursing homes, while working dogs assist police officers and firefighters. Even the family pet learns a lot, from obeying commands to figuring out how to sneak an extra treat when no one's looking.

Despite all their amazing qualities, what makes dogs truly special is their ability to bring people together. Have you ever noticed how a dog can turn strangers into friends? At the park, someone might come up to you just to pet your dog and strike up a conversation. Families bond over their shared love for a furry friend, and communities come together to support local shelters and adoption events. Dogs have a way of reminding us to be kind, patient, and caring —not just to them, but to each other.

Why people love and care for dogs.

There's something magical about coming home to a dog. The moment you walk through the door, there they are, wagging their tail like they've been waiting for you all day. It doesn't matter if you've been gone for five minutes or five hours; to a dog, every reunion is the best moment ever. That kind of enthusiasm is hard not to love. It's one of the many reasons why people form such strong bonds with dogs—they make us feel important, valued, and completely loved.

But what's behind this special connection? Dogs have an incredible way of understanding us. It's not just about the treats we give them or the games of fetch we play. They seem to know when we're happy, sad, or even worried. Imagine you've had a rough day at school, maybe you didn't do so well on a test, or a friend said something that upset you. Your dog doesn't need you to explain anything. They'll come over, nuzzle up to you, and rest their head on your lap, as if to say, "I'm here for you." That kind of comfort is something truly special, and it's a big reason why people care so deeply for their dogs.

Dogs also give us something that's rare in the world: unconditional love. Think about it—your dog doesn't care if you're wearing the coolest clothes or if you spilled spaghetti sauce on your shirt. They don't mind if you got a bad grade or if you didn't feel like going outside to play. They love you just as you are. That kind of loyalty makes people want to take care of their dogs in return, making sure they're happy, healthy, and well-fed.

Caring for a dog isn't just a responsibility; it's an opportunity to build a strong, meaningful relationship. When you take your dog for a walk, you're not just exercising them—you're spending time together, exploring the world as a team. When you teach them tricks, like how to sit or stay, you're learning how to communicate with each other. Even small things, like filling their water bowl or scratching behind their ears, create moments of trust and connection. Dogs depend on us, and taking care of them feels good because we know we're giving back a little of the love they give us.

There's another reason people love dogs—they make life more fun. Dogs bring energy and excitement into our lives in ways nothing else can. A game of fetch in the backyard, a walk through the park, or even just tossing a squeaky toy across the living room can turn a boring day into an adventure. Have you ever tried to keep a straight face when a dog does something silly, like chasing their tail or barking at their own reflection? It's impossible not to laugh. Dogs remind us to enjoy the little things, to play, and to find joy in unexpected places.

Dogs also make us feel safe. Some dogs are natural protectors, always on the lookout for anything unusual. Whether it's barking at the mail carrier or standing close when a stranger walks by, dogs give people a sense of security. Even small dogs can be surprisingly fierce when they think their family needs protection. For centuries, dogs have been guarding homes, farms, and even whole communities. That protective instinct is another reason why people trust and care for them so much.

Beyond their loyalty and playfulness, dogs have a unique ability to bring people together. Have you ever noticed how easy it is to start a conversation when there's a dog around? Maybe someone stops to pet your dog at the park, or a neighbor shares a story about their own furry friend. Dogs create connections between people. They help families bond, too. Walking the dog together, training them to do tricks, or even laughing at their goofy antics can strengthen relationships and create shared memories. Dogs aren't just part of a family—they often become the heart of it.

Of course, loving a dog also means taking care of them when they need us most. Dogs can't tell us when they're feeling sick or tired, but they show it in their own ways. Maybe they don't want to play as much, or they seem a little slower than usual. Being there for them during those times is a way of showing how much we care. It's not always easy, but the love we give to dogs always feels worth it. People know that caring for their dogs is a way of saying "thank you" for all the ways dogs make our lives better.

And then there's the fact that dogs are just amazing in so many ways. They've been by our sides for thousands of years, helping us hunt, herd sheep, pull sleds, and even rescue people in emergencies. Today, they're still doing important jobs, like guiding people who are blind or helping firefighters search for survivors after a disaster. Knowing how much dogs do for us makes it impossible not to appreciate them.

Dogs also teach us valuable lessons. They show us what it means to live in the moment. Have you ever noticed how excited a dog gets over the simplest things, like a new toy or a tasty treat? They remind us to appreciate life's little joys. They also teach us patience—training a dog takes time, and learning to understand them can sometimes be a challenge. But through it all, they show us that love, trust, and kindness are what matter most.

1

A BRIEF HISTORY OF DOGS

Thousands of years ago, long before there were golden retrievers fetching balls or dachshunds snoozing on couches, there were wolves. Wild, untamed, and perfectly adapted to their environment, wolves roamed forests, plains, and mountains in search of food. They hunted in packs, communicated with howls, and were some of the most skilled predators on Earth. It might seem hard to imagine that the lovable dogs we know today—snuggling in blankets or begging for treats—share a common ancestor with these fierce hunters, but it's true. Every single dog, from the tiniest Chihuahua to the largest Great Dane, can trace its roots back to wolves.

How did that transformation happen? It's a story

that began tens of thousands of years ago, during a time when humans were living in small groups and moving from place to place. These humans were hunters and gatherers, surviving by finding and hunting their food. It's likely that they crossed paths with wolves, who, just like the humans, were always on the lookout for their next meal. This is where things start to get interesting.

Imagine a wolf pack trailing behind a group of humans. The wolves weren't trying to be friendly—they were probably looking for scraps of food. Maybe the humans had left behind bits of meat from a hunt, and the wolves saw an easy opportunity. Over time, some wolves might have realized that sticking close to humans was safer and easier than hunting on their own. Instead of chasing down a deer, they could hang back and scavenge leftovers. These wolves would have been less aggressive, more curious, and more willing to approach humans than their wilder counterparts.

At the same time, humans might have noticed that having wolves around wasn't such a bad thing. Wolves could help keep other predators away, and their keen senses—especially their incredible hearing and sense of smell—made them excellent early warning systems. If a bear or a rival group of humans was nearby, the wolves would know first. Over many years, a relationship began to form. The wolves benefited from being near humans, and the humans benefited from having wolves close by.

Now, not every wolf was cut out for this new way of life. The more aggressive wolves, the ones that didn't like being near humans, stayed wild and kept their distance. But the calmer, friendlier wolves started to stick around. These were the ancestors of dogs. Slowly, over generations, these wolves began to change. They became less fearful of humans, and their bodies and behaviors started to adapt. Their faces became less sharp, their ears floppier, and their tails wagged more often. They started to look more like the dogs we know today.

One of the most important things that happened during this process was the development of trust. Wolves are naturally cautious animals, and with good reason—being too trusting in the wild can get you into trouble. But the wolves that lived near humans learned that not all humans were dangerous. They began to trust the people who fed them, and in turn, the humans began to trust the wolves. This trust laid the foundation for the incredible bond between dogs and humans that we still see today.

Over time, humans started to realize they could do more than just share food with these animals—they could train them. Maybe one of the early wolves learned to bark when strangers approached, or to help herd other animals. Humans likely noticed these behaviors and encouraged them. The wolves that were the best at helping humans were fed and cared for, and their puppies grew up around people. Those puppies were a little different from their wild ancestors, more comfortable with humans and more eager to please.

As thousands of years passed, these early dogs became more specialized. Humans bred them for specific traits, like speed, strength, or intelligence. In some areas, dogs were bred to help hunt, tracking animals with their incredible noses and retrieving them after a successful hunt. In others, they were bred to protect livestock, staying with sheep or cattle and keeping them safe from predators. Some dogs were bred to be fast runners, others to pull heavy loads, and still others to simply be good companions.

This process, called domestication, is what turned wolves into dogs. But domestication didn't happen overnight. It took thousands of years for humans and dogs to shape each other's lives. In fact, humans changed just as much as dogs did. Living with dogs taught humans how to communicate in new ways, how to form partnerships, and even how to work together toward shared goals.

One of the most fascinating parts of this story is how much of it is still a mystery. Scientists have studied ancient dog bones, DNA, and fossils to piece together the story of domestication, but there are still many questions. For example, when exactly did wolves become dogs? Some researchers believe it happened around 15,000 years ago, while others think it could have been as long as 40,000 years ago. Where did it happen? Some think it began in Asia, while others argue for Europe or the Middle East. The truth is, it may have happened in multiple places, with different groups of humans and wolves forming bonds at different times.

How Dogs Became "Man's Best Friend"

To understand how this special relationship began, you have to think back to a time when life was much harder for humans. There were no grocery stores or refrigerators. People had to hunt for food, find safe places to sleep, and protect themselves from wild animals. Living was a constant challenge. Wolves, on the other hand, were experts at survival. They were strong hunters with sharp instincts and powerful senses. Humans and wolves didn't start out as friends. In fact, they were probably wary of each other. Wolves saw humans as possible competition, and humans likely saw wolves as dangerous predators.

But something changed. Over time, certain wolves began to linger closer to human groups. These weren't the aggressive, alpha wolves that wanted to rule their pack. Instead, they were the curious, less dominant wolves who figured out that staying near humans might have advantages. Humans left scraps of food behind after meals, and wolves were happy to clean up. This wasn't just convenient for the wolves—it also helped the humans. Wolves that hung around chased off other predators, like bears or large cats, that might have been a threat. They were like an early alarm system, barking or growling if anything dangerous approached.

The wolves that stayed close became more and more comfortable around people. Their pups grew up surrounded by humans, getting used to their sounds, smells, and movements. Those pups were a little different from their wild relatives—less fearful, more cooperative. Over generations, these traits became more pronounced. These early "proto-dogs" were still wolves in many ways, but they were on the path to becoming something new.

Humans started to notice just how helpful these animals could be. A wolf that could warn of danger was one thing, but a wolf that could help hunt? That was a game-changer. People began to encourage wolves to stick around, sharing food with the ones that were most cooperative. This wasn't just about survival—it was the beginning of a partnership. Wolves that worked well with humans were fed and cared for, and their offspring were more likely to have those same cooperative traits. Over time, this selective relationship transformed wolves into the first true dogs.

One of the key reasons dogs became "man's best friend" is their unique ability to bond with humans. Unlike many other animals, dogs are naturally social. In the wild, wolves rely on their pack to survive. They work together to hunt, raise their pups, and protect each other. When wolves started living with humans, they treated people like part of their pack. That's why dogs are so good at reading human emotions—they've been doing it for thousands of years.

Scientists have even found that when a dog looks into a human's eyes, both the dog and the human experience a surge of a hormone called oxytocin. Oxytocin is often called the "love hormone" because it's linked to feelings of trust and affection. It's the same hormone that helps mothers bond with their babies. This chemical connection helps explain why dogs and humans feel such a strong bond—it's literally built into our biology.

Dogs became valuable in ways humans had never imagined. They weren't just helpful in hunting or guarding camps; they also became companions. People began to see dogs as more than just tools for survival. They were friends, members of the family. Dogs offered comfort during tough times, joy during happy moments, and a sense of safety every day. This emotional connection grew stronger with each generation, making dogs an essential part of human life.

As humans moved into new environments, dogs adapted right alongside them. In colder regions, humans bred dogs to have thick fur and the strength to pull sleds. In warmer climates, they bred dogs that could handle the heat and help herd livestock. The bond between humans and dogs grew even deeper as they worked together to survive in all kinds of conditions. This partnership wasn't just about humans shaping dogs—it was about dogs shaping humans, too. Working with dogs taught people to communicate better, to be more patient, and to think about the needs of others.

Stories of dogs' loyalty and bravery started to spread. In many cultures, dogs were seen as protectors and guardians. They were celebrated in myths, legends, and even religion. In ancient Egypt, dogs were often depicted in art and were sometimes buried with their owners to accompany them in the afterlife. In Greek mythology, Cerberus, the three-headed dog, guarded the entrance to the underworld. In real life, dogs were just as heroic, saving lives and helping people in countless ways.

The role of dogs in different cultures and societies

Throughout history, dogs have been more than just companions. They've played important roles in cultures and societies all around the world. From helping ancient hunters track their prey to being symbols of loyalty and bravery, dogs have woven themselves into the stories of humanity in incredible ways. Every culture has its own unique connection with dogs, and these relationships tell us a lot about the values and needs of the people who lived with them.

In ancient Egypt, dogs were highly respected. The Egyptians believed that dogs had special powers and were connected to the gods. They even associated dogs with Anubis, the god of the afterlife, who was often shown as a figure with a dog-like head. Dogs were not only loyal companions but also spiritual guides who could protect their owners in life and in death. Wealthy Egyptians often gave their dogs names, like "Brave One" or "Good Shepherd," and some even buried their dogs with them to ensure they'd stay together in the afterlife.

Moving to ancient Greece and Rome, dogs were equally admired but for different reasons. The Greeks viewed dogs as symbols of loyalty and intelligence. They often featured dogs in their myths and legends, like the story of Odysseus, whose dog Argos waited faithfully for his master's return for 20 years. When Odysseus finally came home, disguised as a beggar, Argos recognized him instantly. Even though the dog was old and weak, his loyalty never wavered, and this story became a powerful example of devotion.

The Romans, on the other hand, were all about practicality. They used dogs for protection and work. Large, strong breeds were trained to guard homes, farms, and even military camps. Roman soldiers often brought dogs into battle, where they were used to intimidate enemies or carry messages. But the Romans also appreciated dogs as pets. Wealthy Roman families kept small dogs as companions, treating them almost like children. Archaeologists have found mosaics and paintings from Roman times showing dogs sitting by their owners or playing in gardens, proving just how important they were in daily life.

In Asia, dogs have played vital roles in both practical and spiritual ways. In ancient China, dogs were often seen as protectors. Some breeds, like the Shar Pei and Tibetan Mastiff, were bred to guard homes and livestock from intruders or wild animals. These dogs were known for their strength and bravery, traits that made them highly valued by their owners. But dogs in China weren't just workers—they were also seen as symbols of good fortune. Statues of stone dogs were often placed outside homes and temples to bring luck and ward off evil spirits.

In Japan, dogs were closely tied to tradition and family life. The Akita breed, for example, was considered a symbol of health and happiness. When a child was born, families would sometimes receive a statue of an Akita as a gift to wish the baby a long and healthy life. Akitas were also famous for their loyalty, like the legendary dog Hachiko. Hachiko waited every day at a train station for his owner, even after the man had passed away. That story touched so many people that a statue of Hachiko still stands at the train station today, reminding everyone of the incredible bond between dogs and humans.

In Indigenous cultures across the Americas, dogs were often considered sacred beings. Native American tribes used dogs in many ways, from hunting to pulling sleds. But dogs also had spiritual significance. Some tribes believed that dogs had the ability to travel between the human and spirit worlds, serving as guides for the souls of the dead. They were often included in ceremonies and rituals, treated as respected members of the community.

The relationship between humans and dogs also evolved in the Arctic, where survival depended on teamwork. Arctic dogs, like the Siberian Husky and Alaskan Malamute, were bred to pull sleds across snow and ice. These dogs were incredibly strong and hardy, able to endure freezing temperatures and long journeys. For the Inuit people, dogs were more than just tools—they were partners in survival. The bond between the Inuit and their dogs was based on mutual trust and respect, as both relied on each other to navigate some of the harshest conditions on Earth.

In Europe during the Middle Ages, dogs became symbols of loyalty and status. Noble families often kept hunting dogs, like greyhounds, which were prized for their speed and skill. These dogs were treated with great care, sometimes even eating better food than the servants! Smaller breeds, like spaniels, were kept as lap dogs by royalty and noblewomen, often shown in portraits to emphasize wealth and sophistication. At the same time, working dogs like sheepdogs and mastiffs were crucial for farmers, helping to herd animals and protect livestock from predators.

Even in more modern history, dogs have continued to play important roles in society. During World War I and World War II, dogs were used as messengers, carrying notes between soldiers on the battlefield. They also helped find wounded soldiers and even carried supplies. Famous war dogs like Sergeant Stubby, a pit bull mix, became heroes in their own right, saving lives and boosting morale for the troops. Stubby was so beloved that he received medals and was even invited to meet presidents!

2

DOG BREEDS AROUND THE WORLD

A dog breed is a group of dogs that share specific traits, like size, color, or behavior, because of how humans have carefully selected and bred them over time. Think of it like this: when people needed dogs to do particular jobs—like herding sheep or guarding a home—they bred dogs with the right qualities for those tasks. Over generations, these dogs developed consistent traits, and those traits became part of what defined the breed. Today, there are more than 340 recognized dog breeds worldwide, and each one has its own unique story.

But what makes a dog a breed? To be part of a breed, a dog needs to have certain features that set it apart from other breeds. For example, German shepherds are known for their intelligence, loyalty, and their strong, muscular build. Bulldogs are famous for their wrinkly faces and stocky bodies. These traits aren't random—they've been passed down from one generation to the next through selective breeding. This means people chose dogs with specific qualities they liked and bred them together to create pups that had the same traits.

Breeds aren't just about looks, though. They also include behaviors and instincts. A border collie isn't just a dog with a sleek black-and-white coat; it's a dog with a natural talent for herding. This instinct has been passed down through generations, making border collies some of the best sheepdogs in the world. Similarly, retrievers, like Labradors and golden retrievers, are known for their gentle mouths. This trait makes them excellent at retrieving game during hunts without damaging it—hence the name "retriever."

The idea of creating breeds started thousands of years ago, when humans first began domesticating dogs. In those early days, people weren't thinking about fancy dog shows or purebred pedigrees. They simply wanted dogs that could help them survive. If a person needed a dog to protect their home, they might breed the biggest, most alert dogs they could find. If they needed a hunting partner, they'd look for dogs that were fast and had a great sense of smell. These practical needs led to the development of many of the breeds we know today.

As time went on, people began to appreciate dogs for more than just their usefulness. They started to notice how beautiful and unique dogs could be. This led to the creation of breeds specifically for companionship or appearance. Take the Pekingese, for example. This small, fluffy dog was bred to be a companion for Chinese royalty. Its lion-like mane and regal posture were highly prized, and the breed became a symbol of status and elegance.

In Europe, many breeds were created to help with farming and hunting. The dachshund, with its long body and short legs, was bred in Germany to hunt badgers. Its name even means "badger dog" in German. Meanwhile, in England, terriers were bred to dig out pests like rats and foxes. Their small size and fearless personalities made them perfect for the job.

In other parts of the world, dogs were bred to adapt to specific environments. In the Arctic, for example, breeds like the Siberian Husky and Alaskan Malamute were developed to pull sleds across snowy terrain. These dogs have thick, double-layered coats to keep them warm in freezing temperatures and strong bodies built for endurance. In warmer climates, breeds like the Basenji from Africa were bred to be skilled hunters. Interestingly, the Basenji is sometimes called the "barkless dog" because it makes unique yodel-like sounds instead of barking.

Even though humans created dog breeds to meet their needs, the process wasn't just about work—it was also about personality. Some breeds were developed to be friendly and affectionate, like the Cavalier King Charles Spaniel, which was bred to be a lap dog for European nobility. Other breeds, like the Shiba Inu from Japan, were bred to be independent and adventurous, making them great companions for active people.

One of the most exciting things about breeds is how they continue to evolve. New breeds are still being developed today, often by mixing traits from existing breeds to create dogs with specific qualities. For example, the Labradoodle—a mix of a Labrador retriever and a poodle—was created to be a hypoallergenic guide dog. This shows how the relationship between humans and dogs is always changing, as people find new ways for dogs to fit into their lives.

But it's important to remember that while breeds are fascinating, they don't define everything about a dog. Every dog is an individual with its own personality, regardless of its breed. A German shepherd might love to herd, but it could also be the biggest snuggle bug on the planet. A Chihuahua might be tiny and feisty, but it could also be calm and laid-back. That's the wonderful thing about dogs—they always find ways to surprise us.

Popular Breeds and Their Characteristics

Working Dogs: Built for Action

Let's start with the superheroes of the dog world: working dogs. These breeds were created to help humans in tough jobs like guarding, pulling, and rescuing. They're strong, intelligent, and love having a job to do.

Take the Siberian Husky, for example. Known for their stunning blue or multicolored eyes and thick fur coats, huskies were bred to pull sleds across icy terrain. They're fast, powerful, and have incredible endurance, which makes them perfect for life in snowy regions. But don't let their serious work ethic fool you—they're also known for being playful and friendly.

Another impressive working breed is the Saint Bernard. Originally from the snowy Alps, Saint Bernards were famous for rescuing travelers trapped in avalanches. With their massive size and gentle nature, they're like furry giants with hearts of gold. Imagine being lost in a snowstorm and seeing a Saint Bernard coming to your rescue. It's no wonder they're considered heroes.

Then there's the Doberman Pinscher, a sleek and athletic breed often used as a guard dog. Dobermans are incredibly loyal and protective, making them excellent companions for people who need a watchful friend. They're fast learners and always ready to spring into action.

Toy Breeds: Small but Mighty

On the other end of the spectrum are toy breeds—tiny dogs with big personalities. These dogs may be small enough to fit in your lap, but they often have the confidence of a lion.

Take the Chihuahua, for instance. These pint-sized pups might weigh only a few pounds, but they make up for it with their bold and sassy attitudes. Chihuahuas are known for their loyalty to their owners and their knack for stealing the spotlight wherever they go.

Another popular toy breed is the Pomeranian. With their fluffy coats and fox-like faces, Pomeranians look like little balls of fluff. Don't be fooled by their cute appearance—they're full of energy and love being the center of attention. They're also surpris-

often learning tricks and commands

And who could forget the Yorkshire Terrier, or Yorkie? These tiny dogs were originally bred to catch rats in England's textile mills, but they quickly became beloved companions. Yorkies are feisty, affectionate, and always up for an adventure, whether it's exploring the backyard or snuggling on the couch.

Herding Dogs: Masters of the Flock

Herding dogs are like the farmers of the dog world. They were bred to help manage livestock, like sheep and cattle, and they have natural instincts that make them incredible workers.

One of the most famous herding breeds is the Border Collie. These dogs are often called the smartest breed in the world, and it's easy to see why. Border Collies can learn complex tasks and even understand hundreds of words. With their boundless energy and intense focus, they're happiest when they have a job to do. Watching a Border Collie herd sheep is like watching an artist at work—they move with precision and skill, almost as if they're dancing.

The Australian Shepherd, or Aussie, is another herding superstar. Despite the name, this breed actually originated in the United States. Aussies are known for their beautiful multicolored coats and piercing

eyes, often in shades of blue or green. They're inc
ibly energetic and love working with their owners, whether it's herding sheep or competing in agility courses.

Then there's the German Shepherd, a breed that's known for being versatile and hardworking. While they're often seen as police or service dogs, German Shepherds started as herding dogs in Germany. Their intelligence and loyalty make them excellent at almost any task, from guiding people with disabilities to protecting homes.

Sporting Dogs: Partners in Adventure

If you love being outdoors, sporting dogs might be your kind of breed. These dogs were developed to help hunters by retrieving game, pointing out prey, or flushing birds from hiding spots. They're athletic, friendly, and always ready for a new adventure.

The Labrador Retriever is one of the most popular sporting breeds—and one of the most popular breeds overall. Labs are known for their gentle mouths, which makes them perfect for retrieving without damaging what they carry. But they're not just great hunting partners—they're also incredibly friendly and affectionate, making them wonderful family pets.

Golden Retrievers are another favorite. With their shiny golden coats and sweet temperaments, they're often seen as the ultimate "good dogs." Goldens are natural swimmers and love playing fetch, especially if it involves water. They're also famously patient and great with kids.

The English Springer Spaniel is another sporting breed worth mentioning. These dogs are known for their boundless enthusiasm and love for life. Whether they're running through fields or cuddling with their family, Springer Spaniels bring joy wherever they go.

Hounds: Born to Track

Hounds are the detectives of the dog world, bred to track scents or chase prey. They have sharp noses and keen senses, making them experts at solving "mysteries."

The Bloodhound is a perfect example. With their long, droopy ears and wrinkled faces, Bloodhounds have an incredible sense of smell that's unmatched by any other breed. Police and rescue teams often use Bloodhounds to track missing people because they can follow a scent trail for miles.

The Beagle, a smaller member of the hound group, is equally skilled at tracking. Beagles are curious, friendly, and always ready to follow their noses—sometimes to places they shouldn't be! Their playful nature and loving personalities make them fantastic pets for families.

Another standout hound is the Greyhound, known for being one of the fastest dogs on Earth. Greyhounds were bred for speed, and they're often used in racing. But when they're not sprinting, they're surprisingly calm and love lounging around the house.

Terriers: Small but Fearless

Terriers are scrappy little dogs with big hearts. They were bred to hunt pests like rats and foxes, and their tenacious nature makes them fearless.

The Jack Russell Terrier is a classic example. These small, energetic dogs are like little firecrackers, always on the move and ready for action. Jack Russells love to dig, jump, and explore, which makes them perfect for people who enjoy an active lifestyle.

The Scottish Terrier, or Scottie, is another terrier with a bold personality. Known for their distinctive beards and strong wills, Scotties are independent yet deeply loyal to their families.

Unique Breeds and Fun Facts

Have you ever heard of the Xoloitzcuintli? It's a bit of a tongue-twister, but this breed, often called the Xolo for short, is one of the oldest in the world. Originating in Mexico, the Xolo is often hairless, with smooth, dark skin that feels warm to the touch. These dogs were considered sacred by the Aztecs, who believed they could guide souls to the afterlife. Xolos are known for being calm and loyal, making them excellent companions despite their unusual appearance.

Then there's the Norwegian Lundehund, a dog that seems like it could be straight out of a superhero movie. This breed has six toes on each paw and joints that allow them to bend in ways most dogs can't. Why? Lundehunds were bred to climb steep cliffs in Norway to hunt puffins, a type of seabird. Their extra toes and flexible bodies made them perfect for navigating rocky terrain. While they're no longer used for puffin hunting, their agility and unique features make them one of the most fascinating breeds in the world.

If you've ever seen a dog with a lion-like mane, you might have been looking at a Chow Chow. This ancient breed from China is known for its fluffy coat and distinctive blue-black tongue. Chows were originally bred as working dogs, helping with hunting and guarding. They're independent and a bit reserved, but their regal appearance and loyal nature make them unforgettable. The blue-black tongue, by the way, is one of the biggest mysteries about the breed—no one knows exactly why it's that color.

Another standout breed is the Bedlington Terrier, which looks more like a lamb than a dog. With its soft, curly coat and arched back, the Bedlington Terrier is a perfect example of how unique dogs can be. But don't let its gentle appearance fool you—this breed was originally used to hunt rats and other pests. They're quick, agile, and surprisingly tough, despite their delicate looks.

Have you ever seen a dog that resembles a mop? Meet the Komondor, a Hungarian breed famous for its long, corded coat. This coat isn't just for looks—it helps protect the Komondor from harsh weather and predators while guarding livestock. The cords, which can grow incredibly long, require special care, but they make the Komondor one of the most recognizable breeds in the world. These dogs are fiercely loyal and take their role as protectors very seriously.

Speaking of unique coats, the Peruvian Inca Orchid is another hairless breed worth mentioning. Like the Xolo, the Peruvian Inca Orchid has smooth, bare skin and comes in various colors. This breed dates back to ancient Peru, where it was treasured by the Inca civilization. Despite being hairless, these dogs can be surprisingly warm to the touch, and their skin needs extra care to stay healthy. They're playful and affectionate, making them great pets for people looking for something a little different.

Another breed that stands out is the Basenji, often

called the "barkless dog." Instead of barking, Basenjis make a unique yodeling sound known as a "baroo." This breed comes from Africa and was used for hunting in dense forests. Their short coats and slender bodies make them excellent runners, and their sharp minds mean they're always up to something. Basenjis are known for being clean and independent, often grooming themselves like cats.

Then there's the New Guinea Singing Dog, a breed so rare it was once thought to be extinct. These dogs, found in the remote mountains of Papua New Guinea, are known for their musical howls, which sound almost like singing. They're wild at heart but incredibly intelligent and curious. While they're not commonly kept as pets, they're a reminder of the incredible variety in the dog world.

One of the largest breeds in the world is the Irish Wolfhound, a gentle giant that can tower over most humans when standing on its hind legs. Despite their size, Irish Wolfhounds are known for their calm and friendly nature. They were originally bred to hunt wolves, which is how they got their name. Today, they're more likely to be found lounging around with their families, winning hearts with their kind eyes and majestic presence.

On the smaller end of the spectrum is the

Pekingese, a breed that was once reserved for Chinese royalty. These little dogs have long, flowing coats and an air of importance. In ancient times, only members of the imperial family were allowed to own them. Pekingese were often carried in the sleeves of robes, earning them the nickname "sleeve dogs." They might be small, but their personalities are anything but—these dogs are confident, proud, and deeply devoted to their owners.

Let's not forget the Pharaoh Hound, a breed that looks like it stepped straight out of ancient Egyptian art. With its sleek body, pointed ears, and amber eyes, the Pharaoh Hound has a regal appearance that matches its name. Interestingly, when these dogs get excited, their noses and ears blush a rosy pink. This breed is known for its speed and hunting skills, as well as its affectionate and playful nature.

For a truly ancient breed, look no further than the Saluki, often called the "royal dog of Egypt." Salukis were bred for their speed and grace, making them excellent hunters. Their slim bodies and silky coats give them an elegant appearance, and their loyalty to their families is unmatched. They were so highly valued in ancient times that they were often mummified and buried alongside their owners.

3

UNDERSTANDING DOG BEHAVIOR

When you see a dog wagging its tail, it's hard not to smile. That swish-swish motion seems to scream happiness, like the dog is saying, "Hey, I'm really glad you're here!" But is that all a wagging tail means? Not exactly. A dog's tail is like a little flag that communicates all kinds of emotions, from excitement to nervousness. To understand why dogs wag their tails, you have to take a closer look at how they use them to talk.

Most of the time, we think of tail wagging as a sign of happiness, and often it is. If you've ever come home to a dog after being away for a while, you've probably seen their tail going wild. It's wagging so hard it might look like the dog's whole back end is wagging, too! This is a clear sign that the dog is excited to see you.

Their tail becomes a way to say, "You're back! This is the best moment ever!"

But not all wagging tails mean the same thing. The position of the tail and the way it moves can tell you a lot about what a dog is feeling. For example, if a dog's tail is wagging low and slow, it might mean they're unsure or nervous. They're not unhappy, but they're not entirely comfortable either. On the other hand, a tail wagging high and fast often means excitement or confidence. It's like the dog is showing off, saying, "Look at me, I'm ready for anything!"

Sometimes, tail wagging can even be a warning. If a dog's tail is stiff and wagging slowly, it could mean they're feeling tense or unsure about a situation. This type of wag isn't playful—it's a sign that the dog is on alert and might need some space. That's why it's so important to look at the whole picture, including the dog's body language and the situation they're in, to understand what they're trying to say.

Did you know that dogs even wag their tails differently when they're around other dogs? When two dogs meet, their tails become a form of social communication. A friendly dog might wag their tail in a relaxed, loose way, signaling that they're open to interaction. If the other dog wags back in a similar way, it's like they're saying, "Okay, let's be friends!" But if one dog's tail is stiff and barely wagging, it might mean they're feeling cautious or even a little nervous about the encounter.

Scientists have even discovered that dogs wag their tails to the left or the right depending on how they're feeling. A tail wagging more to the right often means positive emotions, like happiness or excitement. A wagging tail that leans more to the left might indicate stress or uncertainty. Isn't it amazing how much information can be packed into a simple tail wag?

It's not just about emotions, though. Tails are also incredibly useful for balance and movement. If you've ever watched a dog running at full speed or making a sharp turn, you might have noticed how their tail acts like a rudder. It helps them stay steady and change direction without tumbling over. This is especially important for breeds that are built for speed, like greyhounds, or for working dogs that need to move quickly and precisely.

Some breeds even have tails that are specially designed for their jobs. For example, retrievers like Labradors use their thick, powerful tails as "rudders" when they're swimming. This helps them steer and move efficiently in the water, which is essential when they're retrieving objects during a hunt. Similarly, herding breeds like border collies use their tails to help them balance as they dart around sheep or cattle. It's like their tails are an extra tool to help them do their job.

What about dogs with curly tails or no tails at all? Curly-tailed breeds like pugs or Shiba Inus often carry their tails in a way that adds to their charm, but they still use them to communicate. Even a little wiggle of a curled tail can signal excitement or interest. For dogs without tails, like some Australian shepherds or Doberman Pinschers, body language becomes even more important. They might rely on their ears, posture, and facial expressions to communicate what other dogs would show with their tails.

The history of tail wagging goes back to when dogs were still wolves. In a wolf pack, tails are essential for communication. A high, wagging tail shows dominance and confidence, while a tucked tail signals submission or fear. As dogs evolved alongside humans, they kept their tails as a way to communicate, not just with other dogs but with people too. It's one of the ways they've adapted to life with humans, making it easier for us to understand what they're feeling.

Even puppies start wagging their tails at a young age, usually when they're a few weeks old. At first, they only wag when they're around their mom or siblings. It's like their way of saying, "I'm here! Let's play or cuddle!" As they grow, they start wagging more in response to people and new experiences. Watching a puppy wag its tail for the first time is one of the sweetest things you'll ever see.

While wagging tails are wonderful, it's important to remember that not all dogs use their tails in the same way. Some dogs wag all the time, while others only wag in specific situations. Every dog is different, just like every person is different. Learning to understand what a dog's tail is telling you is part of building a strong relationship with them.

How Dogs Communicate

If you couldn't talk, how would you tell someone you were excited, nervous, or even scared? You might jump up and down, wave your hands, or maybe make some noises like a cheer or a shout. Dogs face this challenge every day—they don't use words, but they still manage to communicate with us and each other in ways that are clear and powerful. From barking to growling to how they move their bodies, dogs have an entire language that's fascinating to learn.

Let's start with barking. Barking is probably the first thing people think of when they imagine how dogs communicate. It's their way of grabbing attention, like saying, "Hey, look at me!" But not all barks mean the same thing. If you pay close attention, you'll notice that the tone, pitch, and speed of a bark can tell you a lot about what the dog is trying to say.

For example, a high-pitched, rapid bark might mean excitement. Imagine a dog at the door, barking happily when their owner comes home. It's like they're shouting, "You're back! You're back!" On the other hand, a deep, slow bark can be a warning, like when a dog senses a stranger approaching. This kind of bark says, "I see you. Don't get too close."

Some barks are playful and inviting, like when a dog barks while wagging its tail and lowering its front paws into a playful bow. This kind of bark says, "Let's have some fun!" Other times, barking might signal frustration, like when a dog is trying to get your attention for something they want, such as dinner or a trip outside. It's their version of saying, "Hurry up!"

Growling, on the other hand, is often misunderstood. Many people think a growl always means a dog is angry, but that's not entirely true. Growling is a way for dogs to express a range of emotions, and it's important to understand the context. Sometimes, a growl is a warning, like when a dog feels threatened or uncomfortable. They're saying, "I need space, please don't push me."

But growling isn't always about being upset. Dogs sometimes growl during play, especially when they're having a tug-of-war with a toy. This playful growl sounds different from a warning growl—it's less intense and doesn't come with the same stiff body language. It's as if the dog is saying, "This is fun! Let's keep going!" Knowing the difference between these types of growls is key to understanding what a dog is feeling.

While barking and growling are important, a dog's body language often says even more. Dogs use their entire bodies to communicate, from the tips of their ears to the way they hold their tails. One of the first things to look at is their posture. A relaxed dog will stand or lie down in a loose, easygoing way, with their tail and ears in a neutral position. This means they're calm and comfortable.

A stiff or tense posture, on the other hand, can be a sign that a dog is feeling stressed or unsure. If a dog freezes in place and stares directly at something, they might be deciding what to do next. This could mean they're on alert, and it's a good time to give them space.

Another important clue is the position of a dog's ears. Ears that are forward and upright often mean the dog is focused or curious, like when they hear an interesting noise or see something new. Ears that are flattened back against the head usually signal fear or submission. It's their way of saying, "I'm not a threat, please don't hurt me."

A dog's mouth also tells a story. A relaxed, slightly open mouth with the tongue hanging out usually means the dog is happy and comfortable. But a tightly closed mouth or lips pulled back to show teeth can be a sign of stress, fear, or aggression. Sometimes, dogs will even yawn or lick their lips when they're feeling anxious. These are subtle signals that can help you understand how a dog is feeling in a situation.

Let's not forget the eyes. A dog's eyes can be incredibly expressive. Soft, relaxed eyes with slow blinking are a sign of trust and comfort, while wide, staring eyes with a lot of the whites showing—often called "whale eye"—can indicate fear or discomfort. If a dog avoids making eye contact altogether, they might be feeling submissive or unsure.

One of the clearest ways dogs communicate is through their tails, as you learned earlier. But the tail isn't the only part of their body language that's important. The way a dog moves can also say a lot. A dog that's bouncing around with playful energy is inviting you to join in the fun. A dog that's slinking low to the ground with their tail tucked might be scared or trying to avoid conflict.

Dogs even use their noses to communicate. When two dogs meet, they often start by sniffing each other. This might look strange to humans, but it's like a handshake for dogs. By sniffing, they can learn a lot about each other—age, gender, and even what the other dog ate for breakfast! It's their way of saying, "Nice to meet you. Who are you?"

Sometimes, dogs communicate without making any noise at all. Have you ever seen a dog gently nudge someone's hand or rest their head on a lap? These quiet actions can speak volumes. A nudge might mean, "Pay attention to me," while a head resting on you often says, "I trust you and want to be close."

Fun Facts About Dog Intelligence

Did you know that some dogs can understand hundreds of words? One of the most famous examples is a border collie named Chaser, who learned the names of over 1,000 objects. Chaser could fetch specific toys when asked, even if they were mixed in with a pile of others. But what's even more amazing is how she could figure out new words through elimination. For example, if she knew the names of all her toys except one, she'd assume the new name must belong to the unfamiliar toy. That's a level of reasoning that's rare in animals—and it shows just how sharp a dog's brain can be.

While not every dog will know 1,000 words, many can still learn a lot. The average dog is believed to understand about 165 words, including names, commands, and even some phrases. Have you ever noticed how your dog perks up when you say, "Want to go for a walk?" or "Time for dinner!"? It's not just the tone of your voice they're picking up on—they actually recognize the words. And if you've ever tried to spell out "W-A-L-K" to keep them from getting too excited, you know how quickly they catch on!

But intelligence isn't just about words. Dogs are also amazing problem solvers. Some breeds, like border collies, poodles, and German shepherds, are known for their problem-solving abilities. They can figure out how to open doors, get treats out of tricky containers, or navigate obstacle courses with ease. Have you ever watched a dog work on a puzzle toy? They'll sniff, paw, and nudge it until they figure out how to get the treat inside. It's like watching a furry little engineer at work.

Another fascinating aspect of dog intelligence is their ability to read human emotions. Dogs are experts at picking up on subtle cues, like the tone of your voice or the expression on your face. If you're feeling sad, your dog might come over and rest their head on your lap, offering comfort without needing to be asked. Scientists have even found that dogs can recognize emotions in people just by looking at their faces. They're one of the few animals that can do this—and it's a big reason why the bond between humans and dogs is so strong.

Dogs are also great at working together with humans to solve problems. This is something researchers call "social intelligence." For example, if you point at something, a dog will often follow the direction of your finger to figure out what you're trying to show them. This might not seem like a big deal, but it's a skill that even some primates, like chimpanzees, struggle with. Dogs have evolved to pay close attention to human gestures and body language, making them amazing partners for tasks like hunting, herding, and search-and-rescue missions.

Speaking of search-and-rescue, some dogs are trained to use their intelligence and incredible sense of smell to find people in emergencies. Bloodhounds, for example, have noses so sensitive they can track a scent trail that's days old. These dogs aren't just following a general smell—they're picking up tiny particles unique to the person they're searching for. It's like having a superpower, and it's all thanks to a combination of intelligence and natural ability.

But intelligence in dogs isn't just about work—it's also about play. Play is actually a sign of intelligence because it shows creativity and the ability to understand social rules. If you've ever seen two dogs playing together, you might have noticed how they take turns chasing each other or wrestling. They're not just running around randomly—they're following a kind of unspoken agreement that makes the game fun for both of them.

Different breeds of dogs have different kinds of intelligence. For example, working breeds like border collies and German shepherds excel at learning commands and performing tasks. Hound breeds, like beagles and dachshunds, are masters of following their noses to track scents. Terrier breeds are known for their determination and problem-solving skills, especially when it comes to digging or finding hidden objects. Even toy breeds, like Chihuahuas and Pomeranians, show their smarts through their ability to bond closely with humans and learn tricks.

One of the most interesting things about dog intelligence is that it's not just about being clever—it's also about being in tune with people. This is something researchers call "emotional intelligence." Dogs have an incredible ability to understand what we need from them, whether it's a comforting cuddle or an energetic game of fetch. They're also great at adapting to different situations, like figuring out when it's time to be calm and when it's okay to be playful.

Puppies start showing signs of intelligence from a very young age. Even at just a few weeks old, they begin learning from their environment and their littermates. They figure out how to play, how to communicate with each other, and how to interact with people. By the time they're old enough to go to their new homes, they've already learned a lot about how to navigate the world.

Training is one of the best ways to tap into a dog's intelligence. Teaching a dog commands, tricks, or even games like hide-and-seek helps challenge their brain and keeps them mentally stimulated. It's also a great way to strengthen the bond between you and your dog. Dogs love learning because it gives them a sense of purpose and accomplishment. And let's be honest—it's pretty fun to show off a dog that can shake hands, roll over, or fetch specific toys by name!

But intelligence isn't just about what dogs can do—it's also about how they think. Studies have shown that dogs can experience emotions like happiness, fear, and even jealousy. They can remember past events, solve problems, and make decisions based on what they've learned. For example, if a dog knows that barking at the doorbell makes someone come to the door, they might bark to get attention even when there's no one outside. That's not just instinct—that's using logic to get what they want.

4

CARING FOR A DOG

Every dog needs food to stay healthy and happy, but feeding a dog isn't as simple as just filling up their bowl. What you feed your dog and how much you give them can make a big difference in their life. Just like people, dogs need the right balance of nutrients to grow strong, stay active, and feel their best. Whether it's a tiny Chihuahua or a giant Great Dane, every dog's nutritional needs are unique.

Protein is one of the most important parts of a dog's diet. It helps build and repair muscles, keeps their coat shiny, and provides energy. Many dog foods use animal-based proteins like chicken, beef, fish, or lamb. Some even include eggs, which are a great source of protein too. Dogs also need fats in their diet to keep their skin healthy and to give them energy for all their running, jumping, and playing. Ingredients like fish oil or chicken fat provide the healthy fats that dogs need.

Carbohydrates, like rice, potatoes, or oats, are another important part of a dog's diet. They give dogs the energy they need for their daily adventures. Fruits and vegetables, such as carrots, sweet potatoes, or blueberries, can also provide essential vitamins and antioxidants. These ingredients not only taste great to dogs but also help support their immune system, keeping them healthy.

But not all foods are good for dogs. Some human foods can be dangerous or even toxic. Chocolate, grapes, onions, and garlic are a few examples of things dogs should never eat. It's also important to be careful about how much food you give them. Overfeeding can lead to obesity, which can cause serious health problems like joint pain, diabetes, or heart disease. Underfeeding, on the other hand, can make a dog weak and undernourished.

How much food a dog needs depends on their size, age, and activity level. Puppies, for example, need more calories and nutrients than adult dogs because they're growing fast. A puppy might need to eat three or four times a day, while an adult dog usually only needs two meals. Active dogs, like those that run or play a lot, need more calories than dogs that spend most of their time relaxing. Reading the feeding guidelines on a dog food package can help, but it's also a good idea to talk to a veterinarian to make sure your dog is getting the right amount.

Water is just as important as food. Dogs should always have access to fresh, clean water. Their bodies need water to digest food, regulate their temperature, and keep their organs working properly. If a dog doesn't drink enough water, they can become dehydrated, which can make them feel tired and sick. On hot days or after exercise, it's especially important to make sure they're drinking enough.

Some dog owners choose to make their dog's food at home. This can be a great way to ensure your dog is getting high-quality ingredients, but it's also a lot of work. Homemade diets need to be carefully planned to include all the nutrients a dog needs. Without the right balance, dogs can develop health problems. For example, a diet that's too low in calcium can lead to weak bones, while too much fat can cause obesity. If you're thinking about making homemade food for a dog, it's important to work with a veterinarian or pet nutritionist to create a proper recipe.

Treats are another part of a dog's diet, but they

should be given in moderation. Dogs love treats, whether they're crunchy biscuits, chewy sticks, or bits of meat. Treats can be a great way to reward a dog during training or to show them affection, but they shouldn't make up more than 10% of a dog's daily calories. Giving too many treats can lead to weight gain, and some treats, like those made for humans, can be unhealthy for dogs.

Chewing is a natural behavior for dogs, and giving them the right things to chew on can be good for their teeth. Dental chews, for example, can help reduce plaque and tartar buildup, keeping a dog's mouth healthy. But it's important to choose safe chew toys and treats. Hard bones or rawhide can sometimes cause choking or damage a dog's teeth, so it's always a good idea to supervise a dog while they're chewing.

Every dog is different, and their nutritional needs can change over time. Older dogs, for instance, often need food that's easier to digest and lower in calories. Dogs with health conditions, like allergies or sensitive stomachs, might need special diets too. A veterinarian can help recommend the best food for a dog's specific needs, ensuring they stay healthy and happy at every stage of life.

Exercise and Playtime

Different dogs need different amounts of exercise. A border collie, for example, is like a marathon runner. These dogs were bred to herd sheep, which means they have tons of energy and need lots of time to run, jump, and think. On the other hand, a bulldog is more of a couch potato. Bulldogs are perfectly happy with shorter walks and a bit of play, but they don't need hours of exercise like a collie does. Knowing what your dog needs is the first step in making sure they get the right amount of activity.

Walking is one of the simplest and best ways to exercise a dog. It doesn't matter if you live in a big city or a small town—there's always somewhere to take a walk. A daily walk gives your dog a chance to stretch their legs, sniff around, and explore the world. But it's more than just physical exercise; it's also a mental workout. Every new smell or sound is like a puzzle for their brain, keeping them curious and engaged.

Some dogs, especially younger or more active breeds, need more than just a walk. Running, hiking, or playing fetch can help them burn off extra energy. Fetch is a classic for a reason—it's easy to play, and most dogs absolutely love it. A tennis ball, a stick, or even a frisbee can provide hours of fun. If you have a big backyard or a park nearby, fetch is a great way to let your dog run to their heart's content while you get to stay in one spot.

Then there are activities like agility training, where dogs navigate through obstacle courses. This isn't just for show dogs—it's an amazing way to combine exercise with mental stimulation. Dogs get to climb, jump, and weave through poles, all while working closely with their owner. Even if you don't have access to a fancy course, you can set up your own at home using things like hula hoops, cones, or cardboard boxes. Watching your dog figure out the obstacles is as rewarding for you as it is for them.

If you're near water, swimming is another fantastic option. Many dogs, like retrievers and spaniels, are natural swimmers. They love diving into lakes, ponds, or even a kiddie pool in the backyard. Swimming is especially good for older dogs or dogs with joint problems because it's low-impact but still provides great exercise. Just make sure the water is safe and clean, and always keep an eye on your dog while they're swimming.

Playtime isn't just about physical activity—it's also a chance for you and your dog to bond. Games like tug-of-war, hide-and-seek, or even teaching them new tricks are perfect for building trust and communication. Tug-of-war, for example, can be a fun way to let your dog use their strength, but it's also a game of boundaries. Let your dog win sometimes to keep it exciting, but make sure they know when it's time to stop if they get too excited.

Hide-and-seek is another game that dogs love. You can hide behind furniture, in another room, or even outside, and call your dog to come find you. This taps into their natural hunting instincts and keeps their mind sharp. You can also hide toys or treats for them to sniff out, turning playtime into a mini-adventure.

Interactive toys are great for dogs who need a challenge. Puzzle feeders or treat-dispensing toys keep them busy while also rewarding them for solving problems. These toys are especially helpful for dogs that stay home alone during the day, giving them something fun to do while you're away.

But not all play has to be structured. Sometimes, just rolling around on the floor with your dog or letting them chase you around the yard can be just as fun. Dogs live in the moment, and they'll appreciate any time you spend playing with them, no matter how simple it is.

Of course, it's important to make sure your dog stays safe during exercise and play. Always check the environment for anything that could be dangerous, like sharp objects, toxic plants, or busy streets. On hot days, avoid exercising during the hottest part of the day, and make sure your dog has plenty of water to stay hydrated. In colder weather, be mindful of icy sidewalks or snow that could stick to their paws. For dogs with thin coats, like greyhounds, a doggy sweater can help keep them warm.

Pay attention to your dog's signals during playtime. If they seem tired, start panting heavily, or lie down, it's time to take a break. Dogs don't always know when to stop, especially if they're having fun, so it's up to you to make sure they don't overdo it.

Not all dogs enjoy the same kinds of activities, and that's okay. Some dogs are more independent and might prefer exploring the yard or sniffing around on their own. Others are social butterflies and love playing with other dogs at the park. Getting to know your dog's personality will help you find the activities they enjoy the most.

Grooming Tips

Grooming might not be as exciting as playing fetch or going for a walk, but it's one of the most important ways to take care of a dog. Imagine if you never brushed your hair, clipped your nails, or took a bath.

You'd probably feel pretty uncomfortable, right? Dogs need grooming for the same reasons—to stay clean, healthy, and comfortable. And while some dogs need more grooming than others, every dog benefits from a little extra care.

Let's start with brushing. Whether a dog has long, silky fur or a short, smooth coat, regular brushing helps keep their skin and fur in great shape. For dogs with long hair, like golden retrievers or Afghan hounds, brushing helps prevent tangles and mats. Mats can be painful, pulling on the dog's skin and causing irritation. Using a slicker brush or a comb with wide teeth is a good way to keep their fur looking smooth and shiny.

Even short-haired dogs, like boxers or beagles, need brushing. Their fur might not tangle, but brushing helps remove loose hair and dirt while spreading natural oils that keep their coat healthy. A soft-bristle brush or grooming mitt works well for these dogs and gives them a nice massage at the same time. Most dogs love being brushed once they get used to it. It's like a mini spa day, and it's a great way to bond with them.

Some breeds have very thick double coats, like huskies or Samoyeds. These coats are designed to protect the dog in extreme weather, but they also shed a lot—especially during seasonal changes. If you've ever seen what looks like a snowstorm of fur in your house, you know what shedding season is like. Using an undercoat rake or de-shedding tool can help manage all that loose fur and keep the dog feeling cooler and more comfortable.

Bathing is another essential part of grooming, but dogs don't need baths as often as humans do. In fact, too much bathing can strip away the natural oils in their skin, leaving it dry and itchy. Most dogs only need a bath every few weeks, unless they get into something smelly or messy. When it's bath time, using a dog-specific shampoo is important. Human shampoo can irritate a dog's skin because it's not made for their pH balance. Some dog shampoos even have special ingredients, like oatmeal or aloe, to help soothe sensitive skin.

Bathing a dog can be an adventure, especially if they're not used to it. Some dogs love splashing around in water, while others will try to climb out of the tub the moment they get wet. Having everything ready before you start—like shampoo, a towel, and a non-slip mat—can make the process smoother. Talking to your dog in a calm, cheerful voice can also help them feel more relaxed.

After a bath, drying is just as important. For

smaller dogs, a towel might be enough to soak up the water, but larger dogs might need a bit more. Using a pet-safe blow dryer on a low, cool setting can help dry their fur faster, especially if they have a thick coat. Be sure to avoid blowing air directly into their face or ears —it's loud and can be scary for them.

Speaking of ears, cleaning them is an important part of grooming that's often overlooked. Dogs' ears can trap dirt, wax, and even moisture, which can lead to infections if not cleaned regularly. Breeds with floppy ears, like cocker spaniels or basset hounds, are especially prone to ear problems because their ears don't get much airflow. Using a dog-safe ear cleaner and a cotton ball (not a cotton swab) can help gently remove debris. If a dog's ears have a bad smell or look red and irritated, it's a sign to check with a veterinarian.

Nail trimming is another grooming task that might make some dog owners nervous, but it's very important for a dog's health. Overgrown nails can cause pain and even make it hard for dogs to walk properly. If you've ever heard a dog's nails clicking on the floor, it's probably time for a trim. Using a dog nail clipper or grinder can help keep their nails at a healthy length. The key is to avoid cutting the "quick," a sensitive part of the nail that contains blood vessels and nerves. If you're not sure where the quick is, it's better to trim just a little at a time. Some dogs are a bit wiggly during nail trims, so offering treats and praise can help them stay calm.

Let's not forget about a dog's teeth. Dental care is an important part of grooming that keeps their breath fresh and their mouth healthy. Plaque and tartar can build up on a dog's teeth, leading to gum disease or tooth loss if not addressed. Brushing a dog's teeth with a dog-safe toothbrush and toothpaste can make a big difference. Human toothpaste is a no-go because it contains ingredients that can be harmful to dogs. If brushing isn't an option, dental chews or water additives can also help maintain oral health.

Some dogs need extra grooming depending on their breed. Poodles, for instance, have curly coats that require regular trims to keep them from becoming overgrown. Many owners take their poodles to professional groomers for haircuts, but brushing and bathing at home are still important. Other breeds, like schnauzers or terriers, might need their coats "stripped," which involves removing dead hairs to keep the coat looking neat.

Even dogs with minimal grooming needs, like greyhounds, benefit from occasional brushing and baths. Grooming isn't just about appearance—it's also a chance to check for anything unusual, like lumps, bumps, or cuts. It's a time to make sure their skin is healthy and their fur is free of fleas or ticks.

The Importance of Regular Vet Visits

Think about how much dogs do for us every day. They make us laugh, keep us company, and even help us feel better when we're sad. Taking them to the vet is one way we can give back to them. Regular checkups help catch health issues before they become serious. Even if your dog seems perfectly fine, they might have problems you can't see, like dental disease, joint pain, or even heart issues. Veterinarians are trained to spot these things early, giving your dog the best chance at staying healthy.

One of the first reasons to take your dog to the vet is for vaccinations. Vaccines protect dogs from serious illnesses like rabies, distemper, and parvovirus. These diseases can be deadly, but the good news is that they're also preventable. Puppies usually start getting their vaccines when they're a few weeks old, and adult dogs need booster shots to keep them protected. Your vet will create a vaccine schedule tailored to your dog's needs, making sure they're safe no matter where they go.

Another important part of regular vet visits is checking your dog's weight. You might not think much about it, but keeping a dog at a healthy weight is one of the best ways to ensure they live a long life. Being overweight can lead to problems like joint pain, diabetes, or heart disease, while being underweight might mean your dog isn't getting the nutrition they need. Your vet can help you figure out the right diet and portion sizes for your dog, especially if they need to lose or gain weight.

During a checkup, the vet will also examine your dog's teeth. Dental health is often overlooked, but it's a big part of a dog's overall well-being. Plaque and tartar buildup can lead to gum disease, which can cause pain, bad breath, and even problems with eating. If left untreated, it can affect a dog's heart and kidneys, too. Regular dental cleanings and at-home care, like brushing their teeth or giving them dental chews, can make a huge difference. Your vet will let you know if your dog needs extra help with their teeth.

Another thing vets check is your dog's ears. Dogs with floppy ears, like cocker spaniels, or dogs that spend a lot of time swimming are more likely to get ear infections. During a visit, the vet will look for redness, swelling, or an unpleasant smell, which could mean there's an infection. Catching it early can save your dog from a lot of discomfort and make treatment much easier.

Vets also check for parasites like fleas, ticks, and worms. These tiny pests might not seem like a big deal at first, but they can cause serious problems for dogs. Fleas can lead to itchy skin and allergic reactions, while ticks can carry diseases like Lyme disease. Worms, like heartworms or roundworms, can affect a dog's organs and make them very sick. Regular flea and tick preventatives, as well as heartworm medication, are essential, and your vet can recommend the best ones for your dog.

Spaying or neutering is another important part of a dog's health care, and it's something your vet will discuss with you. Spaying (for female dogs) and neutering (for male dogs) not only prevent unwanted puppies but also reduce the risk of certain cancers and infections. For example, spayed females are less likely to get uterine infections or breast cancer, while neutered males are less likely to develop prostate problems. Your vet will help you decide the best time to schedule the procedure based on your dog's age and breed.

One of the best things about regular vet visits is that they give you a chance to ask questions. Maybe you've noticed your dog scratching more than usual, or they're acting a little differently. Maybe you're not sure if their diet is working or if they're getting enough exercise. Vets are there to help you figure these things out and offer advice tailored to your dog's specific needs.

Even as dogs get older, vet visits become even more important. Senior dogs are more likely to develop conditions like arthritis, kidney disease, or vision problems. They might need special diets, supplements, or medications to keep them comfortable. Regular checkups can help catch these issues early, giving your dog a better quality of life as they age.

Of course, some dogs might not be thrilled about going to the vet. The sights, smells, and new faces can be a little overwhelming. If your dog gets nervous, there are ways to make the experience easier for them. Bringing their favorite blanket or toy can help them feel more secure, and speaking to them in a calm, reassuring voice can go a long way. Many vets are also trained to work with anxious dogs, using treats or gentle handling to help them feel more comfortable.

5

TRAINING YOUR DOG

Training your dog isn't just about teaching tricks like "sit" or "roll over." It's about building a bond, keeping your dog safe, and making sure they understand how to live happily in your home. Dogs don't come with a set of rules—they rely on you to guide them, just like you rely on your teacher or parents to show you the way. Training helps your dog know what to expect and how to behave, and it makes life better for both of you.

Think about how excited dogs get when they see something new. They might bark at the doorbell, jump on a visitor, or chase after a squirrel without a second thought. While those things might seem funny or harmless at first, they can quickly become overwhelming—or even dangerous. Training helps your dog learn how to channel that energy into positive behaviors. For example, instead of barking when the doorbell rings, they can learn to sit calmly until the guest comes in. It's like giving them a toolbox full of good choices.

One of the most important reasons to train your dog is safety. Imagine walking your dog outside and they suddenly see a cat across the street. Without training, they might dash after it, not realizing a car is coming. But if they've been trained to come when called, you can stop them in their tracks. Commands like "stay," "leave it," and "heel" can keep your dog safe in situations where they might otherwise get hurt.

Training also strengthens the bond between you and your dog. When you spend time teaching them, you're not just helping them learn—you're building trust. Dogs want to please their humans, and when they succeed, it makes them feel proud. Think about how happy they look when you say "Good dog!" after they've done something right. Training is like a language that helps you and your dog understand each other better.

Positive reinforcement is one of the best ways to train a dog. This means rewarding them when they do something good, rather than focusing on what they do wrong. Rewards can be anything your dog loves: treats, praise, or even a favorite toy. For example, if you're teaching your dog to sit, you'd give them a treat every time they follow the command. Over time, they'll learn that sitting when you say "sit" gets them something great, and they'll be eager to do it again.

Consistency is key when it comes to training. Dogs learn best when everyone in the family uses the same words and rules. If one person says "down" to mean "lie down" and another says "off," your dog might get confused. It's important to agree on what commands you'll use and stick to them. Repetition also helps. The more you practice a command, the more your dog will understand and remember it.

Training sessions don't have to be long or complicated. In fact, short sessions of about 5–10 minutes are often more effective, especially for puppies or high-energy dogs. Dogs can get bored or distracted if a session drags on too long, so keeping things short and fun is the best way to keep their attention. End each session on a positive note, even if it's just asking them to do something simple like "sit" and rewarding them for it.

Puppies are like little sponges—they soak up information quickly, which makes them great learners. Starting training early helps set good habits that will last a lifetime. Teaching a puppy not to jump on people, for instance, is much easier than trying to break that habit once they're a full-grown dog. But it's never too late to train a dog. Older dogs might take a little longer to learn, but they're just as capable of understanding new commands.

Socialization is another important part of training, especially for puppies. This means exposing them to different people, places, and experiences in a positive way. A well-socialized dog is less likely to feel scared or overwhelmed by new situations. Taking your dog to a park, introducing them to friendly dogs, or even letting them hear new sounds like vacuum cleaners or thunder can help them feel more confident in the world.

Some behaviors take time and patience to change, especially if a dog has been doing them for a while. For example, a dog that pulls on the leash might need weeks of practice to learn to walk calmly by your side. The key is not to get frustrated. Dogs can sense your emotions, and staying calm and encouraging will help them feel more secure.

Training isn't just about teaching commands—it's also about understanding why dogs behave the way they do. For instance, a dog might chew on shoes or furniture because they're bored or teething, not because they're trying to be "bad." Redirecting their energy to something positive, like a chew toy, is often more effective than scolding them. Understanding what motivates your dog and meeting their needs makes training much easier.

Some dogs love to learn more advanced skills, like agility or scent work. Agility training involves teaching dogs to navigate obstacle courses, while scent work taps into their natural ability to sniff out specific scents. These activities are not only great exercise but also an excellent way to challenge your dog's mind. Even simple tricks like "shake," "spin," or "play dead" can be fun for both of you.

Basic Commands Every Dog Should Know

Teaching your dog basic commands is like giving them a set of tools to navigate the world. These commands help them understand what's expected and keep them safe, and they also make your life together more enjoyable. Whether it's "sit" to keep them calm, "stay" to keep them out of trouble, or "come" to call them back to you, basic commands are the foundation of good communication with your dog.

Let's start with "sit." This is often the first command people teach their dogs because it's simple and useful. Imagine you're getting ready to feed your dog, and they're bouncing around with excitement. Asking them to sit gives them a clear task to focus on, making it easier for both of you. To teach "sit," hold a treat close to your dog's nose and slowly move it upward and back over their head. As they follow the treat with their eyes, their bottom will naturally lower to the ground. The moment they sit, say "sit" and give them the treat. Over time, they'll learn to associate the word with the action.

Next is "stay," which is all about teaching patience. "Stay" is especially helpful in situations where you need your dog to wait, like when you're answering the door or crossing a busy street. Start by asking your dog to sit, then hold your hand out like a stop sign and say "stay." Take one small step back, then return to your dog and reward them if they stayed in place. Gradually increase the distance and the time you ask them to stay, always rewarding them when they succeed. It's important to go slowly—asking for too much too soon can confuse your dog.

"Come" is another essential command, and it could even save your dog's life one day. Imagine your dog slips out of the yard or runs after a squirrel. Knowing they'll come back to you when called can make all the difference. To teach "come," start in a quiet, distraction-free space. Get down to your dog's level, call their name, and say "come" in a happy, excited voice. You can also clap your hands or pat your legs to encourage them. When they come to you, reward them with treats, praise, or playtime. Practice this often, gradually adding more distractions as they get better.

"Down" is another useful command that helps calm your dog and keep them out of trouble. This is particularly helpful when you need your dog to settle in one spot, like during a family dinner or when guests are visiting. To teach "down," hold a treat in your hand and let your dog sniff it. Slowly lower your hand to the ground, encouraging your dog to follow it. When their chest touches the floor, say "down" and give them the treat. Some dogs might find this command tricky, so be patient and break it into smaller steps if needed.

Teaching "leave it" is all about safety. Dogs are naturally curious, and they often sniff or grab things that aren't good for them, like dropped food or objects on the ground. "Leave it" helps you stop them before they get into trouble. Start by holding a treat in your closed hand and letting your dog sniff it. When they stop sniffing or pawing at your hand, say "leave it" and give them a treat from your other hand. Once they understand the command, practice with treats or objects placed on the floor, making sure to reward them for ignoring the temptation.

"Drop it" is a companion to "leave it," and it's just as important. If your dog picks up something they shouldn't have—like a sock or a stick—you need to be able to get it back without a game of tug-of-war. To teach "drop it," offer your dog a toy or object they like to hold, then show them a treat. Say "drop it" as you offer the treat, and when they let go of the object, give them the treat as a reward. Practice this until your dog understands that letting go of something leads to a reward.

"Heel" is a command that teaches your dog to walk calmly by your side instead of pulling on the leash. This makes walks more enjoyable for both of you. Start in a quiet area and hold a treat at your side to keep your dog's attention. Say "heel" and take a few steps forward. If your dog stays beside you, reward them with the treat. Gradually increase the distance you walk and practice in different environments to help your dog stay focused even with distractions.

"Wait" is similar to "stay," but it's often used in shorter, everyday situations. For example, you might use "wait" when you're opening a door and don't want your dog to run out ahead of you. To teach this command, ask your dog to sit, then hold your hand up and say "wait." Open the door just a little, and reward them if they stay in place. If they try to move, gently close the door and try again. Practice this until your dog understands that "wait" means they need to hold still for a moment.

"Watch me" is a helpful command for getting your dog's attention, especially in distracting situations. Hold a treat near your face and say "watch me" as your dog looks at you. Reward them immediately for making eye contact. This command is great for redirecting your dog's focus when they're excited or nervous.

Fun Tricks to Teach Your Dog

Teaching your dog tricks isn't just about showing off at parties—it's a way to keep their minds active, strengthen your bond, and have fun together. Dogs love learning new things, especially when there's a reward at the end. Whether it's a classic like "shake" or something more playful like "spin," tricks give your dog a chance to shine and let their personality shine through.

Let's start with "shake." This is one of the most popular tricks, and it's a great way to introduce your dog to the fun of learning. To teach "shake," have your dog sit in front of you. Hold a treat in your hand and let your dog sniff it. Then, gently tap or lift their paw while saying "shake." As soon as they lift their paw, even a little, reward them with the treat and lots of praise. Over time, your dog will learn to offer their paw when you say the word. It's like a doggy handshake, and it always gets a smile.

Another fun trick is "spin." This one is perfect for energetic dogs who love to move. To teach "spin," hold a treat near your dog's nose and slowly move it in a circle. As your dog follows the treat, they'll naturally turn in a circle. Once they complete the spin, say "spin" and give them the treat. After a few tries, they'll start to connect the word with the action. You can even teach them to spin in both directions by using commands like "spin left" and "spin right."

"Roll over" is another classic trick that's sure to impress. Start by asking your dog to lie down. Hold a treat near their nose and slowly move it to the side of their head, encouraging them to turn onto their side. Once they're on their side, move the treat in a circle, guiding them to roll onto their back and then back onto their other side. When they complete the roll, say "roll over" and reward them. This trick might take a little patience, but once they get it, it's always a crowd-pleaser.

If your dog is a natural performer, "play dead" is a great trick to try. Start by asking your dog to lie down. Hold a treat near their nose and move it to the side, just like you did with "roll over." As they start to roll onto their side, say "bang" or "play dead" and give them the treat when they're lying still. You can add a dramatic flair by pointing your finger like a pretend gun or saying the command in a playful tone. This trick is fun and shows off your dog's ability to stay still.

For dogs who love to jump, teaching them to "jump through a hoop" is a fun challenge. Start by holding a hula hoop on the ground and encouraging your dog to step through it. Use treats to lure them and reward them once they're on the other side. Gradually raise the hoop a little higher as they get comfortable, always rewarding them for making it through. With practice, your dog will be leaping through the hoop like a pro.

"Fetch" is more than just a game—it's a great way to teach your dog to follow commands. Start by choosing a toy your dog loves, like a ball or a stuffed animal. Toss it a short distance and encourage your dog to go after it. When they pick it up, call them back to you using the "come" command. If they drop the toy before reaching you, gently encourage them to bring it all the way. Once they're close, say "drop it" and offer a treat as a reward. Over time, your dog will learn the full sequence of fetching, returning, and dropping the toy.

If your dog is extra clever, you can teach them "tidy up." This trick involves training your dog to pick up their toys and put them in a basket or box. Start by teaching them to pick up a toy and hold it. Once they've got that down, place the basket nearby and use a treat to guide them to drop the toy into it. Reward them every time they succeed. Gradually add more toys and encourage them to clean up their play area. It's a useful trick that also gives them a job to do.

Teaching your dog to "wave" is another adorable trick. Begin by teaching them "shake." Once they've mastered it, hold your hand just out of reach and say "wave." When they lift their paw but can't reach your hand, reward them. Over time, your dog will learn to lift their paw as if they're waving hello or goodbye.

For dogs who are motivated by food, "balance a treat" is a fun challenge. Ask your dog to sit or lie down, and then gently place a treat on their nose. Say "wait" to keep them still, and after a few seconds, release them with "okay" or "take it." They'll likely flip the treat into their mouth with a quick snap. It takes practice and patience, but once they learn, it's a trick that's always entertaining to watch.

If you're feeling adventurous, you can teach your dog to "speak" and "quiet." To teach "speak," wait for your dog to bark naturally, then say "speak" and reward them immediately. Once they've connected the command with barking, you can use "quiet" to teach them to stop barking. Say "quiet" and reward them when they stop. This trick is especially useful for dogs who bark a lot, as it teaches them to bark on command and stay quiet when asked.

Patience and Positive Reinforcement

Dogs don't learn by magic. They learn through repetition and rewards, which is why patience is such an important part of the process. Let's say you're teaching your dog to sit. The first few times, they might look at you like they have no idea what you want. That's okay! They're just figuring things out. If you get frustrated or raise your voice, it can confuse or scare them, and that slows down the learning process. Staying calm and positive, even when progress is slow, helps your dog feel safe and motivated.

Positive reinforcement is one of the most effective ways to train a dog. It means rewarding your dog for doing something right, rather than punishing them for getting it wrong. Imagine being in school and getting a gold star every time you answered a question correctly. That's what positive reinforcement feels like to your dog. It shows them that good behavior leads to good things, and it makes them want to repeat that behavior.

Rewards can take many forms. Treats are a favorite for most dogs, but praise, petting, or a quick play session with a favorite toy can work just as well. The key is to find out what motivates your dog the most. Some dogs will do anything for a tasty bite of chicken, while others light up at the sound of an enthusiastic "Good job!" Tailoring the reward to what your dog loves makes the training experience even more enjoyable for them.

Timing is everything when it comes to rewards. The closer the reward is to the behavior, the clearer it is to your dog why they're being rewarded. For example, if you're teaching "down," you'll want to give your dog a treat the instant their chest touches the floor. If you wait too long, they might not connect the treat with the action you're teaching. Using a clicker can help with timing. A clicker is a small device that makes a clicking sound when pressed, and it lets your dog know exactly when they've done the right thing. Once they associate the click with a reward, it becomes a powerful training tool.

Mistakes are a natural part of learning, both for dogs and humans. If your dog doesn't get something right away, it doesn't mean they're not smart or that they're being stubborn. It just means they need more time and practice. Breaking the behavior into smaller steps can help. For example, if you're teaching "roll over," start by rewarding your dog for lying on their side. Once they've mastered that, you can build up to the full roll. Celebrating small victories keeps your dog motivated and builds their confidence.

Consistency is another important part of training. If you allow a behavior one day but correct it the next, your dog will be confused about what you want. Imagine if sometimes your teacher let you talk during class but other times got upset when you did. You wouldn't know what to expect, and neither does your dog when the rules aren't clear. Being consistent with commands, rewards, and boundaries helps your dog understand what's expected.

Training is about more than just teaching commands—it's about building a relationship based on trust and understanding. Dogs are incredibly in tune with our emotions, and they look to us for guidance. If you're calm and encouraging, your dog will feel more confident in their ability to learn. On the other hand, if you're impatient or frustrated, they might shut down or act out. Staying positive doesn't mean ignoring mistakes—it means focusing on what your dog is doing right and helping them improve step by step.

It's also important to keep training sessions fun and engaging. Dogs have short attention spans, especially puppies, so short sessions of 5–10 minutes are usually best. If your dog seems distracted or bored, it might be time for a break. Ending on a high note, like rewarding them for a simple command they know well, leaves both of you feeling accomplished and ready for the next session.

Every dog learns at their own pace, and some tricks or commands might take longer to master than others. A border collie might pick up commands quickly because they were bred to work closely with humans, while an independent breed like a Siberian husky might need extra time. That doesn't mean one dog is smarter than the other—it just means they have different ways of learning. Understanding your dog's personality and adjusting your approach makes training more effective and enjoyable.

Distractions can be a challenge during training, especially in busy or noisy environments. Start training in a quiet space where your dog can focus, and gradually introduce distractions as they get better at the command. For example, practice "sit" in your living room before trying it at the park. Rewarding your dog for staying focused in a more challenging environment helps them learn to listen no matter what's going on around them.

6

FAMOUS DOGS IN HISTORY AND POP CULTURE

One of the most famous hero dogs in history is Balto, a Siberian Husky who played a key role in saving lives during the 1925 serum run to Nome, Alaska. At the time, a deadly diphtheria outbreak threatened the small town, and the only cure was a serum located hundreds of miles away. With blizzard conditions making it impossible to use planes or boats, sled dog teams were the only way to deliver the life-saving medicine. Balto led his team through whiteout snowstorms and temperatures so cold that frostbite was a constant danger. Against all odds, they completed their leg of the journey, and the serum arrived in Nome in time to save countless lives. Today, a statue of Balto stands in

New York City's Central Park, reminding everyone of his courage and determination.

Another legendary dog is Hachiko, a Japanese Akita known for his unwavering loyalty. Hachiko belonged to a man named Professor Ueno, who worked at a university in Tokyo. Every day, Hachiko would accompany his owner to the train station and wait for him to return in the evening. Tragically, Professor Ueno passed away unexpectedly while at work, but Hachiko continued to wait for him at the station every single day for nearly 10 years. Hachiko's loyalty touched the hearts of people around the world, and he became a symbol of devotion and love. A statue of Hachiko now stands at Shibuya Station, where he waited so faithfully.

Lassie, though a fictional character, was based on the traits of real-life collies known for their intelligence and bravery. The stories of Lassie rescuing children, warning families of danger, and finding help in emergencies have inspired generations. These tales are a tribute to the countless farm dogs who have done similar acts of heroism in real life.

Speaking of bravery, we can't forget about Smoky, a tiny Yorkshire Terrier who became a hero during World War II. Smoky was found by an American soldier in the New Guinea jungle, and she quickly became part of the unit. Despite her small size, Smoky performed tasks that no human could. In one instance, she helped pull communication wires through a narrow, dangerous pipe, saving hours of work and protecting soldiers from enemy fire. Smoky also lifted spirits by performing tricks for troops and visiting wounded soldiers in hospitals. She's remembered as a symbol of courage and the power of a little dog to make a big difference.

Then there's Rin Tin Tin, a German Shepherd who became a Hollywood star after being rescued during World War I. Found as a puppy in a bombed-out kennel in France, Rin Tin Tin was brought to the United States by an American soldier. His agility, intelligence, and charisma made him a natural on screen, and he starred in many films that showcased the bravery and loyalty of dogs. Rin Tin Tin's story reminds us that even in the darkest times, dogs can bring hope and joy.

Real-life hero dogs also include those who have worked in disaster response. Trakr, a German Shepherd police dog, was part of the rescue efforts after the September 11 attacks on the World Trade Center. Trakr helped locate a survivor trapped under rubble for over

24 hours, showing the incredible power of a dog's nose and determination. His bravery earned him international recognition, and he's remembered as one of the many dogs who played a crucial role in those efforts.

In the world of search and rescue, dogs like Barry have become legends. Barry was a Saint Bernard who worked as a rescue dog in the Swiss Alps over 200 years ago. Known for his ability to find and help travelers stranded in the snow, Barry is credited with saving more than 40 lives during his career. One famous story tells of Barry finding a young boy buried in an avalanche. He licked the boy's face to keep him awake and warm while leading rescuers to the spot. Barry's legacy continues, and Saint Bernards are still used in mountain rescue work today.

Not all hero dogs work in extreme conditions. Some make a difference in everyday life by helping people with disabilities. Buddy, a German Shepherd, was the first guide dog for the visually impaired in the United States. In the 1920s, Buddy helped her owner, Morris Frank, navigate the world with confidence and independence. Morris worked to promote the use of guide dogs, and Buddy's success helped pave the way for thousands of service dogs that assist people to this day.

Dogs like Endal, a Labrador Retriever, show how service dogs can go above and beyond. Endal was trained to assist a veteran with mobility issues, but his intuition and quick thinking saved his owner's life during a medical emergency. When the man collapsed, Endal retrieved his phone, placed it near him, and covered him with a blanket to keep him warm. He even retrieved money from the man's wallet and presented it to passersby to get help. Endal's actions highlight the incredible bond between service dogs and their owners.

Some hero dogs even go into battle to protect their handlers. Cairo, a Belgian Malinois, was part of the Navy SEAL team that carried out the mission to capture Osama bin Laden. These military working dogs are trained to detect explosives, track enemies, and protect their teams in dangerous situations. Cairo's courage and training were vital to the success of the mission, showing how dogs are an invaluable part of even the most challenging operations.

Dogs like Apollo, a search-and-rescue dog who responded to the 9/11 attacks, and Chips, a German Shepherd-Collie mix who served in World War II, remind us of the countless dogs who dedicate their lives to helping others. Whether they're saving people from avalanches, guiding someone safely across a street, or simply offering comfort during tough times, these dogs are true heroes.

Dogs in Movies and TV Shows

One of the most iconic dogs in TV history is Lassie, the brave and intelligent collie who always seemed to know when someone needed help. Lassie's adventures often involved rescuing people in trouble, finding lost items, or even saving the day during emergencies. The show was so popular that it ran for nearly 20 years, making Lassie a household name. Lassie wasn't just a TV character—she became a symbol of loyalty and courage, showing how dogs can be true heroes in our lives.

Another beloved dog from the world of TV is Scooby-Doo, the clumsy but lovable Great Dane who solves mysteries with his human friends. Scooby is known for his love of snacks, his goofy personality, and his catchphrase, "Scooby-Dooby-Doo!" Even though he's often scared of ghosts and monsters, Scooby always finds the courage to help his friends crack the case. With his hilarious antics and heartwarming bravery, Scooby-Doo has been entertaining kids for generations.

In movies, one of the most famous dogs is Toto

from *The Wizard of Oz*. Toto, a little Cairn Terrier, is Dorothy's loyal companion as she journeys through the magical land of Oz. Whether he's barking at the Wicked Witch or helping Dorothy find her way home, Toto proves that even the smallest dogs can play a big role in an adventure. His loyalty and bravery remind us why dogs make such great friends.

Speaking of bravery, who could forget Beethoven, the lovable St. Bernard from the *Beethoven* movies? Beethoven is huge, slobbery, and full of personality. In the films, he gets into all kinds of mischief, from causing chaos in the house to outsmarting villains who threaten his family. Despite his messy antics, Beethoven's heart of gold always shines through. His stories remind us that dogs aren't just pets—they're part of the family.

Another dog that captured hearts on the big screen is Marley from *Marley & Me*. Marley is a Labrador Retriever who is as mischievous as he is lovable. The movie follows his life with his owners, showing both the challenges and the joys of living with such a spirited dog. Marley's story is full of humor, but it's also a touching reminder of the deep bond between dogs and their families.

For fans of adventure, there's Bolt, the white shepherd from the animated movie of the same name. Bolt believes he has superpowers because he's the star of a TV show, but when he gets lost in the real world, he learns what it truly means to be a hero. Along the way, Bolt discovers that his courage and love for his owner, Penny, are his greatest strengths. His journey is a heartwarming mix of action, humor, and friendship.

Another animated favorite is Dug from *Up*. Dug is a Golden Retriever who can talk thanks to a special collar. His goofy, enthusiastic personality and love for his new human friends make him one of the most memorable characters in the movie. Whether he's shouting "Squirrel!" or offering heartfelt loyalty, Dug perfectly captures what we love most about dogs—their ability to bring joy and laughter into our lives.

For a more classic story, there's Old Yeller, a film about a stray dog who becomes a loyal protector for a pioneer family. Old Yeller is brave, smart, and fiercely devoted to his family, risking his life to keep them safe. His story is both heartwarming and bittersweet, showing how dogs can leave a lasting mark on our hearts, even after they're gone.

Dogs in movies and TV aren't just sidekicks—they're often the stars of the show. 101 Dalmatians features a whole pack of spotted pups who outsmart the villainous Cruella de Vil. Led by Pongo and Perdita, the dalmatians show incredible teamwork and courage as they protect their puppies from danger. Their adventure is filled with excitement and humor, making it a favorite for dog lovers everywhere.

Another animated classic is Lady and the Tramp, a tale of two very different dogs who find love despite their differences. Lady, a refined Cocker Spaniel, and Tramp, a scrappy stray, go on an unforgettable journey together, sharing spaghetti in one of the most famous scenes in movie history. Their story shows that love and friendship can come in all shapes and sizes.

In more recent years, movies like *Secret Life of Pets* have given us a playful look at what our pets might be up to when we're not home. Dogs like Max, Duke, and Gidget lead the pack in hilarious and heartwarming adventures, reminding us just how much our furry friends mean to us.

Even superhero movies have their canine stars, like Krypto the Superdog, who is Superman's loyal companion. With his superpowers and heroic heart, Krypto proves that dogs can save the day just as well as their human counterparts. His adventures highlight the special connection between heroes and their pets.

And then there's Hooch, the drooling yet lovable French Mastiff from *Turner & Hooch*. Hooch turns the life of a neat-freak detective upside down, but his loyalty and instincts help solve the mystery at the heart of the movie. Their bond grows stronger with every chaotic moment, showing how dogs can bring out the best in us, even when they challenge us.

Mythical and Legendary Dogs

In ancient Greek mythology, one of the most famous dogs is Cerberus, the three-headed guardian of the underworld. Cerberus was said to guard the gates of Hades, preventing the living from entering and the dead from escaping. Despite his fearsome appearance, Cerberus wasn't all bad. In some myths, he's depicted as loyal to Hades and even gentle to those who approached him respectfully. Hercules, one of the greatest heroes in Greek mythology, once had to capture Cerberus as part of his Twelve Labors. The image of a three-headed dog has fascinated people for centuries, symbolizing strength, vigilance, and the mysteries of life and death.

Moving to Norse mythology, there's Garmr, a fierce hound who is said to guard the gates of Hel, the realm of the dead. Garmr is often compared to Cerberus because of his role as a guardian of the afterlife. In the myth of Ragnarok—the Norse version of the end of the world—Garmr is prophesied to fight in a great battle, representing chaos and destruction. Despite his ominous role, Garmr's story shows how dogs were seen as powerful protectors, even in the darkest of tales.

In Celtic mythology, there are many stories about magical dogs. One of the most famous is Cú Chulainn's hound, also called the Hound of Ulster. Cú Chulainn, a legendary Irish hero, earned his name—which means "Hound of Culann"—after a dramatic encounter with a ferocious guard dog. When Cú Chulainn accidentally killed the hound in self-defense, he offered to take its place as the guardian of Culann's property until a new dog could be raised. This tale highlights the loyalty and courage associated with dogs in Celtic culture.

The Celts also believed in Faerie Dogs, mystical creatures often described as large, ghostly hounds with glowing eyes and green or white fur. These dogs were said to roam the countryside at night, sometimes as protectors and other times as omens of danger. In some stories, they were guides for lost souls, leading them safely to the afterlife. These magical hounds remind us of how people have long viewed dogs as guardians between worlds.

In England, tales of the Black Dog are both eerie and captivating. The Black Dog is often described as a ghostly, shaggy creature with glowing red or yellow eyes. Depending on the story, it might appear as a warning of danger or as a protector against evil. One famous legend is that of the Barghest, a spectral dog said to haunt the countryside in northern England. While these tales might sound scary, they also show how dogs were seen as powerful and mysterious beings capable of influencing the human world.

In Aztec mythology, dogs were deeply respected and believed to play an important role in the afterlife. The Aztecs told stories of Xoloitzcuintli, a breed of hairless dog that was thought to guide the souls of the dead through the underworld. These dogs were considered sacred and were often buried with their owners to help them on their journey to the afterlife. The Xoloitzcuintli, or "Xolo" for short, is still a living breed today, and its connection to ancient legends makes it a unique and fascinating part of history.

Chinese mythology includes the story of Panhu, a divine dog who is celebrated as a hero. According to the legend, Panhu was loyal to the emperor and played a key role in defeating the emperor's enemies. As a reward, Panhu was transformed into a human and married the emperor's daughter. This tale highlights the idea that dogs possess qualities like bravery, intelligence, and loyalty that make them worthy of great honor.

In Japanese folklore, there are stories of Inugami, or "dog spirits," which were believed to serve as guardians or even bring good fortune to families. Inugami were said to be powerful and fiercely loyal, but they could also be mischievous if not treated with respect. These stories reflect the deep respect the Japanese people have for dogs as protectors and companions.

In Native American folklore, dogs often appear as symbols of protection, guidance, and unconditional love. Some tribes tell stories of dogs acting as spiritual guides, helping humans navigate through challenges or warning them of danger. In other tales, dogs are messengers between the physical and spiritual worlds, reinforcing the idea that they are more than just earthly companions.

In Indian mythology, the Sarama is a divine dog mentioned in the Rigveda, one of the oldest sacred texts. Sarama is described as loyal and wise, serving as a messenger for the gods. In later Hindu mythology, dogs are associated with Yama, the god of death. They are believed to guard the gates of the afterlife and protect the souls of the departed. This dual role of protector and guide shows how deeply dogs are woven into the spiritual beliefs of many cultures.

Even in modern legends, mythical dogs capture

our imagination. The story of Greyfriars Bobby from Scotland, for example, has taken on a legendary quality. Bobby, a Skye Terrier, is said to have spent 14 years guarding the grave of his owner in Edinburgh. While Bobby was a real dog, his story has grown into a symbol of loyalty and devotion that feels almost mythical.

7

FUN DOG FACTS AND TRIVIA

Let's start with the biggest dog ever recorded. That title goes to Zeus, a Great Dane from Otsego, Michigan. Zeus stood an unbelievable 44 inches tall at the shoulder—that's over 7 feet tall when he stood on his hind legs! Zeus was so big that his food bowl had to be placed on a table, and he could drink water straight from the kitchen sink. Despite his enormous size, Zeus was a gentle giant, known for his friendly and loving personality.

On the other end of the scale is the smallest dog ever, a tiny Chihuahua named Miracle Milly. Milly measured just 3.8 inches tall, about the size of a soda can! She was so small that her owners had to feed her with an eyedropper when she was a puppy. Even as an adult, Milly weighed only about a pound, but her big personality made her unforgettable.

Speed is another area where dogs shine. The title of fastest dog breed goes to the Greyhound, and for good reason. Greyhounds can reach speeds of up to 45 miles per hour, making them the cheetahs of the dog world. But when it comes to the fastest recorded dog, that honor belongs to a Greyhound named Star Title, who clocked an incredible 50.5 miles per hour during a race. Watching a Greyhound run is like seeing poetry in motion—they're built for speed, with long legs, a sleek body, and a powerful stride.

While Greyhounds are known for their speed, the record for longest jump by a dog belongs to a Whippet named Spitfire. Whippets are cousins of Greyhounds and are also incredibly fast and agile. Spitfire amazed everyone by jumping a whopping 31 feet in a dock diving competition. Imagine jumping the length of a school bus—that's how far Spitfire leaped!

Some dogs break records with their intelligence and skills. Chaser, a Border Collie, is known as the world's smartest dog because she learned the names of over 1,000 objects. Her owner, a retired professor, worked with her daily to teach her new words, and Chaser could fetch specific toys based on their names. She could even understand sentences and combine commands, showing just how intelligent dogs can be when they're given the chance to learn.

Speaking of intelligence, did you know there's a record for the most tricks performed by a dog in one minute? A talented Border Collie named Striker holds that title, completing an amazing 49 tricks in just 60 seconds. From jumping through hoops to balancing objects, Striker's lightning-fast moves show how much dogs can achieve with training and practice.

Not all records are about speed or size. Some celebrate dogs' unique talents. Take Mochi, for example, a Saint Bernard with the longest tongue on a dog. Mochi's tongue measures an incredible 7.31 inches! She uses her record-breaking tongue for everything from giving slobbery kisses to enjoying her favorite treats.

Dogs also hold records for their loyalty and dedication. A Labrador Retriever named Endal became famous for his ability to assist his disabled owner with everyday tasks. Endal could fetch items, operate buttons, and even use an ATM card! He holds the record for the most tasks performed by a service dog, proving just how life-changing these amazing animals can be.

When it comes to endurance, one dog stands out: a Border Collie named Jumpy holds the record for the fastest 100-meter run by a dog on two legs. Jumpy trained tirelessly with his owner and completed the run in just 19.33 seconds. Whether running on his hind legs or performing other tricks, Jumpy's energy and skill left everyone in awe.

Some dogs break records with their appearance. For example, a sheepdog named Colonel holds the title for the longest fur on a dog. His luxurious coat measures over 11 inches long, giving him a majestic look that turns heads wherever he goes. Grooming Colonel is no small task, but his owner takes pride in keeping his record-breaking fur looking fabulous.

Another standout is Bluey, an Australian Cattle Dog who holds the record for the oldest dog ever recorded. Bluey lived to an astonishing 29 years and 5 months, which is more than twice the average lifespan of most dogs. His long life is a testament to the care and love his family gave him, as well as the resilience of this hardworking breed.

Not all record-breaking dogs are about individual achievements. Some make history as part of a team. For example, the largest gathering of dogs wearing bandanas took place in Japan, where 764 dogs came together to show off their stylish accessories. Events like this celebrate the fun and joy that dogs bring to our lives, as well as the community of dog lovers around the world.

Even tricks as simple as catching a ball can lead to records. Purin, a Beagle, holds the record for the most balls caught by a dog with their paws in one minute—14 in total! Watching Purin catch ball after ball is like seeing a canine version of a pro basketball player. Her focus and agility make her an absolute star.

And then there's the story of Finley, a Golden Retriever who holds the record for the most tennis balls held in a dog's mouth at once. Finley can carry an incredible six tennis balls at the same time! It's a hilarious sight to see, but it also shows the determination and fun-loving nature of dogs.

The Science Behind a Dog's Sense of Smell

A dog's sense of smell is up to 100,000 times more powerful than ours. This means they can detect things that are completely invisible to us. The reason for this incredible ability lies in their noses, which are specially designed for sniffing. When a dog takes a sniff, the air doesn't just go in and out the way it does for us. Their nose has two separate airways—one for breathing and one just for smelling. This allows them to keep sniffing while they breathe, which is part of what makes them such amazing scent detectors.

Inside a dog's nose are hundreds of millions of scent receptors—way more than what humans have. To give you an idea, we have about 5 million scent receptors in our noses, while a dog like a Bloodhound can have up to 300 million. That's why a Bloodhound can track a scent trail days after it was made, even if it's been raining. It's like they're following a glowing path that only they can see.

But the nose is just part of the story. The way a dog's brain processes smells is equally amazing. A dog's brain has a special part called the olfactory bulb that's dedicated to processing scents. This part of their brain is about 40 times larger, proportionally, than the same part of a human brain. In fact, scientists estimate that dogs dedicate about 12% of their brain to analyzing smells, compared to just 1% in humans. It's as if their brain is built to be a smell-detecting machine.

Dogs don't just smell things—they can also break smells down into layers. Imagine walking into a pizza shop and smelling a delicious pizza baking. To you, it smells like one big, amazing scent. But a dog can smell each ingredient separately: the cheese, the tomatoes, the oregano, the crust. This is why dogs are so good at finding specific scents, whether it's a piece of missing evidence in a crime scene or a tiny crumb of food hidden under a couch.

One of the most incredible things about a dog's sense of smell is its ability to detect things that aren't even visible. For example, dogs can smell changes in human emotions. When you're scared or nervous, your body releases certain chemicals, like adrenaline, and a dog can pick up on those tiny changes. This is why some dogs are trained as therapy or emotional support animals—they can sense when their owners are upset and offer comfort.

Dogs can also smell things happening inside the body. Certain medical alert dogs are trained to detect illnesses like cancer or low blood sugar in people with diabetes. They can even warn someone of an oncoming seizure. Scientists aren't entirely sure how dogs do this, but it's believed that they can detect changes in the body's chemistry that we can't even measure yet.

Another mind-blowing ability is how dogs use their sense of smell to navigate. While we rely on maps or GPS, dogs can use scent trails to find their way. For instance, a dog that gets lost miles away from home can often sniff their way back by following the faint scents they left behind on their journey. It's like they have an invisible map stored in their noses.

Tracking isn't just about following one scent, either. Dogs can pick out individual smells in a crowded environment. Imagine a dog working in an airport, where there are thousands of people, bags, and food smells all mixed together. That dog can still detect the specific scent of explosives or drugs, proving just how sharp their noses are. This is why dogs are so valuable in jobs like search and rescue, law enforcement, and even conservation work.

Some breeds are particularly famous for their sense of smell. Bloodhounds, for example, are often used in tracking because their long ears and wrinkled faces help trap scents around their noses. German Shepherds and Belgian Malinois are commonly used in police and military work because they combine a strong sense of smell with intelligence and focus. Labrador Retrievers, meanwhile, are popular as detection dogs for finding everything from missing people to bedbugs.

But even a regular pet dog has an incredible nose. Ever noticed how your dog seems to know when you've been around another dog, even if you don't smell like one? That's because they can detect the tiniest scent particles left on your clothes or skin. It's their way of keeping track of what's happening in their world.

Dogs also use their noses to communicate with each other. When two dogs meet, the first thing they usually do is sniff each other. This isn't just about saying hello—it's how dogs gather information. They can learn a lot about another dog just from a quick sniff, like their age, gender, health, and even what they've been eating.

Even more fascinating is how dogs use their sense of smell to understand time. While we use clocks and calendars, dogs can tell time through scent. For example, the scent of a person fades over the course of the day, and a dog can use this information to know how long it's been since that person was home. This is why your dog might start waiting by the door at the same time every day—it's not because they know the time on a clock, but because they can "smell" that it's almost time for you to return.

How Dogs Impact Human Health

One of the biggest ways dogs impact human health is by helping us stay active. Think about all the times you've seen people walking their dogs at the park or in the neighborhood. Dogs need daily exercise, which means their owners get exercise, too. Even a short walk can make a big difference for your body. Walking gets your heart pumping, your muscles working, and your lungs breathing fresh air. For many people, the idea of going to the gym sounds boring, but taking a walk or playing fetch with a dog? That's fun!

Dogs also help reduce stress. Have you ever noticed how just petting a dog makes you feel calm? There's actually science behind that. When you spend time with a dog, your brain releases chemicals like oxytocin, sometimes called the "love hormone." Oxytocin makes you feel happy and relaxed, and it lowers your stress levels. At the same time, spending time with a dog can reduce the amount of cortisol in your body. Cortisol is a hormone linked to stress, and having less of it helps you feel more at ease.

Dogs can even make your heart healthier. Studies have shown that people who own dogs often have lower blood pressure and healthier hearts than those who don't. Petting a dog, hearing them breathe, or even just sitting near them can help slow down your heart rate. Some scientists believe that the bond between dogs and humans creates a sense of companionship that's good for your heart—literally!

But it's not just about physical health. Dogs have a huge impact on mental health, too. People who live with dogs often feel less lonely. Dogs are always there for you, whether you've had a great day or a tough one. They're good listeners, even if they don't understand every word, and their wagging tails or excited greetings can turn a bad mood into a good one almost instantly.

For people with anxiety or depression, dogs can be life-changing. Therapy dogs are specially trained to comfort people who are feeling sad, anxious, or overwhelmed. They might visit hospitals, nursing homes, or schools to bring comfort to people who need it. These dogs don't just offer cuddles—they create a calming presence that helps people feel more grounded and secure.

Service dogs go even further in helping humans. These amazing animals are trained to assist people with specific medical or physical needs. For example, guide dogs help people who are blind or visually impaired navigate the world safely. Hearing dogs alert people who are deaf to important sounds, like doorbells or fire alarms. There are even dogs who can detect changes in their owner's body, like drops in blood sugar for people with diabetes, or the onset of a seizure for someone with epilepsy. These dogs save lives every day.

Dogs are also helping in the field of medicine. You

might have heard about dogs being used to sniff out diseases like cancer. Their powerful sense of smell can detect tiny changes in the body that humans can't see or feel. In some cases, dogs have been able to identify cancer in its early stages, giving people a better chance at successful treatment. This isn't just a theory—it's something real dogs are trained to do, and it's making a big difference in how doctors approach certain illnesses.

For kids, growing up with a dog can have incredible health benefits. Studies have shown that children who live with dogs are less likely to develop allergies or asthma. Being around a dog exposes kids to different types of bacteria, which helps strengthen their immune system. Plus, playing with a dog encourages kids to be active, which is great for their physical health.

Dogs can also have a positive effect on how kids develop socially and emotionally. Kids who grow up with dogs often learn responsibility by helping to take care of them. Feeding, walking, and grooming a dog teaches important life skills and helps kids understand the importance of caring for another living being. Dogs also help kids develop empathy. When a child comforts their dog or notices how their dog is feeling, they're learning to be more understanding and kind to others.

Even schools are starting to recognize the benefits of having dogs around. Some schools have therapy dogs that help students feel calmer and more focused. Imagine walking into a classroom and seeing a friendly dog waiting to greet you. Just being near the dog can help ease nervousness about tests or tough days. These dogs don't just help students—they brighten the whole school environment.

The connection between dogs and humans doesn't stop at individual health. Dogs are also used in group therapy and community programs to bring people together. For example, veterans who are struggling with PTSD (post-traumatic stress disorder) often find comfort and healing through programs that pair them with dogs. These programs help both the veterans and the dogs, creating a bond that gives both sides a sense of purpose.

Even people who don't own dogs can benefit from spending time with them. Animal shelters often have programs where people can volunteer to walk or play with the dogs waiting to be adopted. These programs don't just make the dogs happy—they also help the volunteers feel better. Spending time with animals is a great way to lift your mood, reduce stress, and even meet new people.

8

HOW TO BE A RESPONSIBLE DOG OWNER

The first thing to consider is why you want a dog. Are you looking for a companion to join you on adventures, or do you want a quiet friend to cuddle with at home? Dogs come in all shapes, sizes, and personalities, so thinking about what kind of dog fits your lifestyle is really important. If you love hiking and being outdoors, a high-energy breed like a Border Collie or Labrador Retriever might be a great match. But if your idea of a perfect day is relaxing on the couch, a laid-back dog like a Bulldog or Basset Hound might be a better fit.

Next, think about how much time you have to spend with a dog. Dogs are social animals, and they need attention, exercise, and training every single day. Puppies, in particular, require a lot of time and patience. They're learning everything for the first time—where to go potty, what's okay to chew on, and how to listen to commands. Training a puppy can be a full-time job for a while. If you're not sure you have that much time, adopting an older dog might be a better option. Older dogs are often already trained and settled, making them great companions for people with busier schedules.

Money is another big part of owning a dog. Dogs need food, toys, grooming supplies, and regular vet checkups, all of which can add up. On top of that, there are unexpected costs, like if your dog gets sick or injured. Being prepared to take care of your dog financially is just as important as being ready emotionally. If you're part of a family, this is something to discuss together, since everyone will be involved in taking care of the dog.

Once you've thought about your lifestyle and resources, it's time to learn about the different breeds or types of dogs. Each breed has its own traits, needs, and quirks. For example, Huskies are beautiful and fun, but they're also super energetic and need lots of exercise. Dachshunds are adorable, but their long backs make them prone to certain health problems. Mixed-breed dogs, often found at shelters, can be wonderful choices, too. They might not come with a specific breed description, but their unique personalities can be just as rewarding.

If you're considering getting a dog from a shelter, you're not just finding a pet—you're giving a dog a second chance at a happy life. Many shelter dogs are loving, loyal, and grateful for the care you provide. Shelters often have dogs of all ages, sizes, and personalities, and the staff can help match you with a dog that fits your family. Plus, adopting from a shelter helps reduce the number of homeless pets, making a difference in your community.

If you decide to get a dog from a breeder, it's important to do your research. Responsible breeders prioritize the health and well-being of their dogs, not just making money. They'll let you meet the puppy's parents, show you where the puppies are raised, and provide health records. Avoid puppy mills or breeders who don't take good care of their dogs, as these places often prioritize profit over the dogs' welfare.

Once you've found the right dog, it's time to prepare your home. Think of it like baby-proofing—dogs are curious and might get into things they shouldn't. Make sure dangerous items like cleaning supplies, electrical cords, or breakable objects are out of reach. Create a safe space for your dog, like a cozy bed or crate, where they can relax and feel secure.

Stock up on essentials like food, water bowls, a leash, and toys to make their transition as smooth as possible.

Training is one of the most important parts of being a dog owner. It's not just about teaching tricks—it's about helping your dog learn how to live in your home and be part of your family. Start with basic commands like "sit," "stay," and "come." These aren't just helpful for you—they also keep your dog safe. Positive reinforcement, like treats and praise, works best and helps build trust between you and your dog.

Socializing your dog is equally important. This means exposing them to different people, places, and experiences in a positive way. Socialization helps your dog feel more comfortable and confident, whether they're meeting a new friend or visiting a new park. Puppies, in particular, benefit from early socialization, but it's never too late to help a dog learn to feel at ease in different situations.

Being a responsible dog owner also means understanding your dog's health needs. Regular vet checkups, vaccinations, and parasite prevention are all part of keeping your dog healthy. Spaying or neutering your dog is another important decision that can prevent health problems and reduce the number of homeless animals. Pay attention to your dog's behavior and energy levels—if something seems off, it's always a good idea to check with your vet.

Exercise is a daily must for dogs, but the amount depends on their age, size, and breed. High-energy dogs need plenty of opportunities to run, play, and explore, while smaller or older dogs might be happy with a couple of shorter walks. Mental stimulation is just as important as physical activity. Puzzle toys, training games, and interactive play keep your dog's brain engaged and help prevent boredom.

And, of course, love is at the heart of being a good dog owner. Dogs thrive on affection and attention. Whether it's snuggling on the couch, playing in the yard, or simply spending time together, your dog will cherish every moment with you. They don't need fancy toys or expensive gear—they just need to feel like a valued part of your family.

Adopting vs. Buying a Dog

Adopting a dog is a wonderful way to give an animal a second chance at a happy life. Shelters and rescue organizations are full of dogs waiting for homes. These dogs come in all shapes, sizes, and ages—each with their own personality and story. Some might have been lost, while others were surrendered by owners who couldn't care for them anymore. What all of these dogs have in common is that they're looking for love, stability, and a fresh start.

One of the best things about adopting is knowing that you're making a difference. When you adopt a dog, you're not just giving that one animal a home—you're also creating space in the shelter for another dog in need. It's like a ripple effect of kindness, and it feels amazing to know you're part of that.

Adopted dogs are often just as wonderful as dogs from breeders, but some people worry that shelter dogs might have problems or "baggage." While it's true that some rescue dogs might need extra patience and care, many are simply in need of a stable environment and someone to love them. In fact, shelter staff often work hard to match dogs with families that fit their needs and energy levels. They can tell you if a dog is good with kids, enjoys other pets, or loves playing fetch.

Another thing to consider when adopting is that many shelters spay or neuter the dogs, give them vaccinations, and even microchip them before adoption. This can save you time and money compared to buying a puppy from a breeder. Some shelters also provide resources like training classes or advice on helping your new dog adjust to their home.

If you decide to adopt, be prepared to spend time getting to know the dogs. Most shelters encourage meet-and-greets where you can interact with the dog and see if you're a good match. If you already have pets, some shelters let you bring them along to see how they get along. It's all about making sure the adoption works for everyone involved—especially the dog.

On the other hand, buying a dog from a breeder is another path that some people choose, especially if they're looking for specific traits or breeds. Reputable breeders put a lot of care into raising healthy, well-socialized puppies. They can provide detailed information about the breed's characteristics, energy levels, and potential health issues. If you're looking for a dog to match a particular lifestyle—like a working dog for herding or a small companion for apartment living—a breeder might be able to help you find the right fit.

It's important to do your homework when choosing a breeder. A responsible breeder will prioritize the health and well-being of their dogs over making money. They'll be happy to answer your questions, show you where the puppies are raised, and let you meet the puppy's parents. These breeders often take great pride in their dogs and want to make sure they're going to good homes.

Unfortunately, not all breeders are responsible. Puppy mills are large-scale breeding operations that prioritize profit over the health and happiness of the dogs. Dogs in these facilities are often kept in poor conditions, and their puppies might have health or behavioral issues as a result. Avoiding puppy mills is essential, and one way to do this is by visiting the breeder in person to see how the dogs are cared for.

Another option to consider is breed-specific rescue groups. If you're interested in a particular breed but want to adopt instead of buy, these organizations can help. They rescue and rehome dogs of specific breeds, often from shelters or owners who can no longer care for them. This can be a great way to combine the benefits of adopting with finding the breed you love.

Teaching Kids to Care for Dogs

Dogs and kids are often the best of friends, but teaching kids how to care for a dog goes beyond just playing fetch or sharing cuddles. Caring for a dog is a big responsibility, and getting kids involved helps them learn important skills like empathy, patience, and teamwork. When kids understand what it takes to care for a dog, they don't just become better pet owners—they grow into kinder, more thoughtful people.

The first step in teaching kids to care for a dog is helping them understand that dogs are living creatures with needs and feelings. A dog isn't a toy that can be played with and then forgotten when something else seems more exciting. Dogs rely on their humans for food, exercise, love, and attention. Explaining this to kids in a simple, clear way helps them see that owning a dog is a partnership, not a one-sided relationship.

One way to teach responsibility is to give kids specific tasks they can handle. Feeding the dog is a great place to start. Show them how much food the dog needs and how often they should be fed. For younger kids, this might mean scooping the food into the bowl under your supervision. For older kids, they can take on the full responsibility of keeping the feeding schedule. Letting kids measure out the food themselves also teaches them math skills, like understanding portions.

Walking the dog is another task that many kids enjoy. It's not just a chore—it's a chance to bond with the dog and get outside for some fresh air and exercise. Before letting a child take the leash, make sure they understand how to keep the dog safe. Teach them to always hold the leash firmly, be aware of cars and other animals, and never let the dog eat anything off the ground. If the dog is large or strong, walking might need to be a shared responsibility between an adult and the child.

Grooming is another way kids can help care for a dog, and it's a great opportunity to teach them about hygiene. Brushing the dog's fur is usually a simple and safe task for kids, and most dogs love the attention. Explain how regular grooming helps keep the dog's coat healthy and prevents shedding from getting all over the house. You can also involve kids in giving the dog a bath, though you might want to be ready for a splash zone!

Cleaning up after a dog might not be the most glamorous task, but it's an important one. Teaching kids to pick up after the dog during walks or clean up accidents inside the house helps them understand that being a responsible pet owner isn't always fun and games. For younger kids, this can start as a shared task with an adult until they're ready to handle it on their own.

Training is another great way for kids to be involved. Dogs thrive on positive reinforcement, and kids love seeing the results of their efforts. Teach kids how to give simple commands like "sit" or "stay," and show them how to reward the dog with treats and praise when they follow through. Make sure kids understand that yelling or getting frustrated doesn't work—dogs learn best when they feel safe and encouraged.

It's also important to teach kids about boundaries, both for their safety and the dog's comfort. Explain that dogs don't always want to play, and it's important to respect their space when they're eating, sleeping, or feeling unwell. Show kids how to recognize the signs that a dog is feeling nervous or upset, like growling, showing their teeth, or hiding. Learning to read a dog's body language helps kids build trust and prevents misunderstandings that could lead to accidents.

Helping kids understand the importance of regular vet visits is another part of teaching them how to care for a dog. You can explain that just like people go to the doctor for checkups, dogs need to see the vet to stay healthy. If possible, involve kids in the process by letting them come along to appointments. They can help hold the leash or ask the vet questions, like what the dog's favorite treat might be for good health.

Kids can also learn about nutrition by helping to prepare healthy treats for the dog. There are lots of simple recipes for dog-friendly snacks, like frozen peanut butter and banana bites or baked sweet potato chips. Making these treats together is a fun way to teach kids about healthy eating, and the dog will be thrilled with the results.

Teaching kids about the cost of owning a dog is another valuable lesson. You don't have to overwhelm them with numbers, but explaining that food, toys, and vet visits all cost money helps them appreciate the commitment involved. You can even encourage kids to save up for a special toy or treat for the dog, teaching them about budgeting and planning.

Beyond the daily tasks, kids should also understand that dogs need love and attention to be happy. Spending quality time with the dog—whether it's playing, snuggling, or just sitting together—builds a strong bond. Encourage kids to talk to the dog, read stories to them, or invent games they can play together. These moments create memories that kids will cherish forever.

If your family is adopting a dog, involving kids in the process is a great way to teach them about compassion. Let them help pick out toys or set up the dog's bed before bringing them home. Talk about how the dog might feel nervous or scared in a new environment and how they can help the dog feel safe and welcome. This teaches kids to think about others' feelings and how their actions can make a difference.

Finally, lead by example. Kids learn a lot by watching the adults in their lives, so showing them how to care for a dog responsibly is the best way to teach them. If they see you being gentle, patient, and consistent with the dog, they're likely to follow your lead. Celebrate their efforts, no matter how small, and let them know they're doing a great job.

THE BOND BETWEEN HUMANS AND DOGS

One of the most famous examples of loyalty is the story of Hachiko, a golden Akita from Japan. Hachiko lived in the 1920s with his owner, a professor named Hidesaburo Ueno. Every day, Hachiko would walk with the professor to the train station in Tokyo and wait for him to return in the evening. One day, the professor didn't come home because he passed away while at work. But Hachiko kept going to the station every single day for nearly 10 years, waiting for his beloved owner. He became a symbol of unwavering loyalty, and people in the community cared for him, bringing him food and water. Today, a statue of Hachiko stands at Shibuya Station, where he waited faithfully. His story reminds us how deeply dogs can love.

Another tale of loyalty comes from Scotland, where a small Skye Terrier named Greyfriars Bobby became a legend. Bobby was deeply devoted to his owner, a night watchman named John Gray. After John passed away, Bobby refused to leave his owner's gravesite. For 14 years, Bobby guarded the grave, keeping watch and only leaving for food. The people of Edinburgh were so touched by his devotion that they took care of him, even building a shelter near the grave for Bobby to rest. A statue of Greyfriars Bobby now stands near the cemetery, and his story is celebrated as a testament to a dog's loyalty.

In Alaska, during the early 1900s, a Siberian Husky named Balto became a hero through his bravery and determination. Balto was part of a sled dog team that helped deliver life-saving medicine during a diphtheria outbreak in the town of Nome. The journey was long and treacherous, with blizzards and freezing temperatures making it nearly impossible. Balto led his team through the harshest part of the journey, ensuring the medicine arrived safely. His courage saved countless lives, and his loyalty to his team and mission made him a symbol of heroism. Today, a statue of Balto stands in Central Park in New York City to honor his incredible feat.

The story of Capitan, a German Shepherd from

Argentina, is another touching example of loyalty. After his owner, Miguel Guzman, passed away in 2006, Capitan disappeared from the family home. A week later, Miguel's family found Capitan at the cemetery, lying on Miguel's grave. No one had shown Capitan the location of the grave—he had found it on his own. For over a decade, Capitan stayed by the grave, only leaving to search for food or water. His loyalty amazed everyone, and he became a local legend.

In more recent times, the story of Hawkeye, a Labrador Retriever, touched hearts around the world. Hawkeye belonged to Navy SEAL Jon Tumilson, who passed away during a mission in Afghanistan. At Jon's funeral, Hawkeye walked to the front of the church and lay beside his owner's casket, refusing to leave. The image of Hawkeye lying there became a powerful symbol of a dog's love and loyalty.

Another incredible story is that of Canelo, a dog from Cadiz, Spain, who spent years waiting outside a hospital for his owner. Canelo and his owner had a routine: they would walk together to the hospital for the owner's treatments, and Canelo would patiently wait outside. One day, the owner passed away while at the hospital. Not understanding what had happened, Canelo continued to wait outside every day for over a decade. The townspeople cared for Canelo, bringing him food and water, and they even named a street after him to honor his loyalty.

Dogs aren't just loyal to their owners—they also show devotion to their fellow animals. In one story, a stray dog in India was spotted caring for an injured puppy on a busy road. Despite having no home or owner, the dog stayed with the puppy, protecting it from traffic and searching for food to share. People who witnessed this act of kindness were so moved that they rescued both dogs and found them a loving home together.

The bond between humans and dogs is often strongest in times of danger. During the September 11 attacks in New York City, a guide dog named Roselle led her blind owner, Michael Hingson, down 78 flights of stairs in the World Trade Center. Despite the chaos and fear around them, Roselle stayed calm and focused, guiding Michael to safety. Her bravery and loyalty in such a terrifying situation showed the true strength of the bond between a dog and their owner.

There's also the remarkable story of Bobby, a Collie mix who traveled 2,800 miles to return home to his family. In 1923, while on a family trip in Indiana, Bobby became separated from his owners. The family searched for him but eventually had to return home to

Oregon without him. Six months later, Bobby appeared on their doorstep, thin and tired but overjoyed to be home. His journey across the country, through forests and deserts, stunned everyone who heard about it. Bobby's determination to reunite with his family showed just how strong the connection between a dog and their humans can be.

How Dogs Help People

Service dogs are specially trained to help people with disabilities or medical conditions live more independent lives. Guide dogs, for example, help people who are blind or visually impaired navigate the world safely. They learn to stop at curbs, avoid obstacles, and even refuse commands if it would put their owner in danger. This is called "intelligent disobedience," and it's one of the most remarkable things about guide dogs. Imagine telling your dog to cross the street, but they stop because a car is coming. It takes incredible focus and training, and it shows how much these dogs care about keeping their owners safe.

Hearing dogs are another type of service dog. They assist people who are deaf or hard of hearing by alerting them to important sounds like doorbells, alarms, or even a baby crying. These dogs often use physical cues, like nudging their owner or leading them to the source of the sound. For someone who can't hear these everyday noises, a hearing dog can make the world feel a lot less overwhelming.

Then there are medical alert dogs, whose sense of smell can literally save lives. These dogs are trained to detect changes in their owner's body that signal a medical problem. For example, diabetic alert dogs can smell when their owner's blood sugar levels drop too low or rise too high. They'll alert their owner by pawing at them or bringing them a special device to check their levels. Similarly, seizure alert dogs can sense when their owner is about to have a seizure and warn them to get to a safe place. Some even learn to stay with their owner during the seizure to keep them calm and safe.

Mobility assistance dogs help people with physical disabilities by performing tasks that might be difficult or impossible for their owners. They can open doors, pick up dropped items, pull wheelchairs, and even help their owner get dressed. Imagine needing your shoes but not being able to reach them—and then your dog brings them to you, tail wagging the whole time. These dogs don't just make life easier; they also give their owners a sense of freedom and confidence.

Post-traumatic stress disorder (PTSD) service dogs

are trained to help people who've experienced trauma, such as veterans or survivors of natural disasters. These dogs provide comfort and security by recognizing signs of anxiety or panic and stepping in to help. For example, a PTSD dog might nudge their owner to interrupt a flashback or lead them out of a crowded area if they're feeling overwhelmed. They're like a steady, reassuring presence in their owner's life.

Therapy dogs, on the other hand, have a different role. Unlike service dogs, they're not trained to assist one specific person. Instead, they visit hospitals, schools, nursing homes, and other places to bring comfort and joy to many people. Imagine being in a hospital bed, feeling nervous or lonely, and then a friendly dog comes trotting in with a wagging tail. Just petting a dog can lower stress, reduce pain, and make you feel happier.

Schools sometimes bring in therapy dogs to help students during stressful times, like exams or big transitions. These dogs aren't doing math homework or giving advice—they're just being themselves, offering a calming presence that makes everything feel a little less scary. Therapy dogs are also wonderful for children with special needs, helping them feel more comfortable and confident.

In nursing homes, therapy dogs can brighten the

day for elderly residents. Many of these people may not have regular visitors or much social interaction, and spending time with a dog can make a big difference. The simple act of stroking a dog's fur can bring back happy memories of pets they've had in the past and create new, joyful moments.

Even airports have started bringing in therapy dogs to help travelers feel less stressed. Flying can be nerve-wracking, especially if there are delays or long lines. Seeing a cheerful Golden Retriever or a playful Labradoodle in the terminal can turn a frustrating day into a much better one.

What makes service and therapy dogs so amazing isn't just their training—it's their natural ability to connect with people. Dogs are incredibly intuitive. They can sense when someone is upset, scared, or in need of comfort, and they respond in ways that humans sometimes can't. A dog doesn't judge, get impatient, or say the wrong thing. They're just there, offering unconditional love and support.

Training these special dogs takes time and dedication. Service dogs usually spend about two years in training before they're ready to work. During this time, they learn specific tasks tailored to the needs of the person they'll assist. Therapy dogs also go through training to make sure they're calm, friendly, and comfortable in a variety of settings. Not every dog is cut out for this kind of work—it takes a unique combination of intelligence, temperament, and love for people.

The bond between a service or therapy dog and the people they help is unlike anything else. It's built on trust, teamwork, and mutual respect. These dogs don't just do their jobs—they go above and beyond to be there for their humans. And in return, the people they help often describe their dogs as life-changing, giving them hope, independence, and a sense of security.

10

THE FUTURE OF DOGS

One of the most fascinating ways dogs are helping scientists is through their incredible sense of smell. A dog's nose is far more powerful than any human-made machine. While we can smell a delicious pizza, a dog can detect every ingredient in that pizza—tomatoes, cheese, flour, spices—layer by layer. Scientists are using this super-scenting ability to study diseases. For example, dogs have been trained to sniff out cancer, sometimes even earlier than traditional medical tests can detect it. Their noses can pick up tiny changes in the chemicals people give off when they're sick, making them valuable allies in diagnosing illnesses.

Dogs are also being trained to detect other health

problems, like Parkinson's disease, malaria, and even COVID-19. During the COVID-19 pandemic, researchers worked with dogs to identify the virus by smell. These dogs could screen people quickly and non-invasively, making them helpful in airports, public events, and other crowded places. Imagine walking past a friendly Labrador who gives you a quick sniff to make sure you're healthy—that's the future scientists are exploring.

Beyond human health, dogs are helping protect the environment. Conservation scientists are working with specially trained detection dogs to find endangered animals and track their populations. These dogs can sniff out animal droppings, also called scat, which contain DNA, diet information, and other clues about the animals' lives. By analyzing scat, scientists can learn about a species without needing to disturb it. For example, dogs have helped track the elusive snow leopard in the Himalayas, a task that would be nearly impossible for humans alone.

In Africa, dogs are helping fight wildlife trafficking. Some dogs are trained to detect ivory, rhino horns, and other illegal wildlife products being smuggled across borders. Their work helps stop poachers and protect endangered species. These dogs are making a huge difference in preserving the planet's biodiversity.

Dogs are even assisting in solving mysteries of the past. Archaeologists have started using detection dogs to locate ancient burial sites. These dogs can sniff out human remains buried for thousands of years, helping scientists uncover new clues about ancient civilizations. Their noses are so sensitive that they can detect scents far below the surface, where even the best technology might struggle.

The bond between dogs and humans is also being studied by scientists interested in behavior and communication. Researchers want to understand how dogs think and how they interpret human emotions. For example, some studies focus on how dogs recognize facial expressions or pick up on subtle changes in tone of voice. This research not only helps us communicate better with our furry friends but also sheds light on the evolution of human-animal relationships.

One area of research explores how dogs might help people with mental health challenges. Scientists are studying how interactions with dogs affect brain chemistry, particularly the release of oxytocin, a hormone associated with happiness and bonding. This research could lead to new therapies for people with anxiety, depression, or PTSD.

Another exciting development is in the field of robotics. Engineers are designing robots inspired by the way dogs move, think, and interact with the world. These "robot dogs" might one day be used in search-and-rescue missions, exploring dangerous areas where it's too risky for humans or real dogs to go. While these robots don't replace real dogs, they highlight how much dogs inspire innovation.

Dogs are also helping scientists understand genetics. By studying the DNA of different dog breeds, researchers are learning about how certain traits develop, such as coat color, size, and behavior. This research isn't just about dogs—it also helps scientists understand human genetics, since dogs and humans share many of the same genetic diseases. For example, studying cancer in dogs can provide clues for developing treatments for humans.

In agriculture, dogs are helping scientists study crop health. Trained dogs can detect diseases in plants before they're visible, giving farmers a chance to save their crops early. This can prevent food shortages and reduce the use of harmful pesticides. It's another way dogs are using their noses to make the world a better place.

The Role of Dogs in Modern Society

One of the most visible roles dogs have today is as service animals. These highly trained dogs are more than just helpers—they're life-changing companions. For people who are blind or visually impaired, guide dogs provide independence and confidence. Imagine crossing a busy street, not knowing where the cars are, and trusting your guide dog to keep you safe. That's the kind of teamwork these dogs bring to their humans.

But service dogs go beyond guiding. For someone with epilepsy, a seizure alert dog might notice small changes in their body and give a warning before a seizure happens. This extra time can mean getting to a safe place or taking medicine before it's too late. For veterans dealing with post-traumatic stress disorder (PTSD), specially trained dogs offer comfort and stability, breaking through moments of anxiety or fear with their calming presence. These dogs aren't just helpful—they're lifesavers.

In schools, therapy dogs are becoming a regular sight. These dogs aren't teaching math or grading papers, but their presence helps students feel less stressed. Whether it's reading a book aloud to a dog or simply sitting next to one during a tough day, kids often find that dogs make school feel safer and more welcoming. Some schools even use therapy dogs during exams to help students stay calm. It's hard to feel overwhelmed when a fluffy, friendly Labrador is wagging its tail nearby.

In hospitals, therapy dogs visit patients to lift their spirits. For someone recovering from surgery or undergoing treatment, a visit from a dog can make a huge difference. Studies show that spending just a few minutes petting a dog can lower blood pressure, reduce pain, and improve mood. These dogs bring more than comfort—they bring hope. And it's not just patients who benefit. Nurses and doctors often find that a dog's visit can brighten their day, too, giving them a much-needed break from their demanding jobs.

Airports are another place where dogs are stepping into new roles. Traveling can be stressful, with long lines, delays, and the chaos of crowded terminals. Enter the "stress-relief dogs." These specially trained therapy dogs wander through airports, letting travelers pet them or just enjoy their calming presence. It's amazing how a simple tail wag can make everything feel a little less hectic.

Dogs are also on the frontlines of security. At airports, borders, and large events, detection dogs are hard at work. Their powerful noses can sniff out explosives, illegal drugs, or even smuggled wildlife. What's remarkable is how fast they can work. A dog can clear a room for safety in just a few minutes, something that would take humans much longer. And because they're non-invasive, people often feel more comfortable around a dog than they would around machines or extra security checks.

In law enforcement, dogs are vital team members. Police dogs help track down missing people, find evidence, and even chase down suspects. Their agility and sense of smell make them perfect for jobs that require speed and precision. In many communities, police dogs are seen as heroes, not just for their bravery but for the bonds they build with their human handlers.

Beyond work, dogs are also becoming more important in family life. As more people live in cities, dogs have adapted to being urban companions. Parks designed specifically for dogs have popped up in cities worldwide, giving them a safe place to run, play, and socialize. For many city dwellers, a dog isn't just a pet—it's a link to the outdoors and a reminder to slow down and enjoy life.

Technology is another area where dogs are playing a role. Researchers are exploring ways to use dogs' natural abilities in new fields, like robotics and artificial intelligence. For example, some robots are being designed to mimic a dog's ability to navigate tricky terrain or respond to human emotions. While these robots won't replace real dogs, they're proof of how much dogs inspire innovation.

In entertainment and media, dogs continue to capture our hearts. From Instagram-famous pups with millions of followers to heartwarming movies about the bond between dogs and humans, it's clear that people can't get enough of them. Dogs remind us of the joy of simple things—a wagging tail, a playful bark, or a comforting snuggle after a hard day.

How We Can Protect and Care for Dogs in the Future

One of the most important ways we can protect dogs in the future is by giving them safe and loving homes. Sadly, millions of dogs around the world don't have families. Many of them live in shelters, waiting for someone to adopt them, while others roam the streets, struggling to survive. In some places, people have started community programs to help these dogs. They set up shelters, provide food and water, and even offer free spaying and neutering to control the number of stray dogs. Supporting programs like these can make a huge difference, giving dogs a chance at a better life.

Adoption is another powerful way to help. When people adopt dogs instead of buying from irresponsible breeders or puppy mills, they're giving a home to an animal in need. But adoption is just the beginning. Being a good pet owner means committing to your dog for their entire life. It means understanding their needs, providing regular vet care, and treating them like a valued member of the family. The more people learn about responsible dog ownership, the better the future will be for dogs everywhere.

Caring for dogs also means protecting their environment. Imagine how many dogs live in cities, sharing space with cars, loud noises, and busy streets. Creating more dog-friendly parks and safe walking areas can give dogs a place to exercise and play without stress. In neighborhoods, people can work together to make their communities safer for dogs, ensuring there are no harmful chemicals, loose wires, or dangerous areas where dogs could get hurt.

Education plays a huge role in protecting dogs. When kids and adults learn about how dogs communicate and what they need, it helps prevent misunderstandings and accidents. For example, not everyone knows how to read a dog's body language. A wagging tail might mean a dog is happy, but it could also mean they're feeling unsure or excited. Teaching people how to interact with dogs safely and kindly can help build stronger, more trusting relationships between dogs and humans.

Another way to protect dogs in the future is by improving their healthcare. Just like people, dogs can get sick, and they need regular checkups to stay healthy. Vaccines, dental care, and parasite prevention are all important, but many dogs don't have access to these basics. Some organizations are working to change that by bringing mobile vet clinics to areas where people can't afford regular veterinary care. These clinics provide free or low-cost treatments, making sure every dog gets the care they deserve.

Technology is also helping dogs in exciting new ways. There are now GPS collars that help owners keep track of their pets, so if a dog ever gets lost, they can be found quickly. Smart feeders ensure dogs get the right amount of food, even if their owners are at work. And there are apps that connect dog owners with trainers, walkers, and even virtual vets. By using these tools wisely, we can make life better for both dogs and their owners.

At the same time, protecting dogs means standing up against cruelty. Sadly, not all dogs are treated with kindness. Animal abuse and neglect are serious problems, and it's up to all of us to speak out when we see a dog in trouble. Many countries have laws against animal cruelty, but enforcing these laws can be tricky. Supporting organizations that rescue abused animals and push for stronger protections can help create a world where no dog has to suffer.

Advocacy for animal rights is another way we can care for dogs. This includes fighting against harmful practices like puppy mills, where dogs are often kept in poor conditions and bred repeatedly without care for their health. By raising awareness and choosing ethical options when adding a dog to the family, people can help shut down these operations.

Conservation efforts also play a role in protecting wild dogs. While many of us think of dogs as pets, there are also wild species like African wild dogs and dingoes that face threats from habitat loss and hunting. Protecting their natural habitats and educating people about their importance to the ecosystem can help these animals thrive.

In the future, it's also important to think about how climate change might affect dogs. Hotter temperatures, stronger storms, and other environmental changes can be tough on animals. For pet dogs, this might mean needing more water, shade, or protection during extreme weather. For stray and wild dogs, it might mean losing access to food and safe shelter. Helping dogs adapt to these changes—and working to slow climate change in the first place—can make a big difference.

CONCLUSION

Dogs are more than just pets. They're companions, protectors, helpers, and even heroes. What makes them truly amazing isn't just one thing—it's a combination of their loyalty, intelligence, and the deep bond they share with humans. Whether they're snuggling on the couch, guiding someone through a busy street, or sniffing out a problem no one else can detect, dogs bring something special into our lives that no other animal can match.

One of the most remarkable things about dogs is how they seem to understand us, often better than we understand ourselves. A dog doesn't need words to know how you're feeling. They can tell when you're happy, sad, or even a little scared, just by watching your body language and listening to your tone of voice. When you're upset, they might rest their head on your lap or nuzzle you with their nose. When you're excited, they'll bounce around, wagging their tail as if to say, "I'm excited too!" It's almost like they have a superpower for sensing emotions, and they use it to make our lives better.

Another thing that makes dogs incredible is their loyalty. Stories of dogs waiting years for their owners or traveling miles to find them aren't just heartwarming—they're proof of how deeply dogs care. This kind of loyalty isn't something you can teach. It's part of who they are. A dog doesn't care what you look like, what kind of day you've had, or whether you've made mistakes. They just love you, unconditionally and wholeheartedly.

Dogs are also brilliant problem-solvers. Think about the many jobs they've taken on over the years: herding sheep, guarding homes, helping law enforcement, and even working with scientists. They don't just follow commands—they figure things out. When a search-and-rescue dog is on a mission, they're not just sniffing around randomly. They're analyzing scents, thinking through obstacles, and using their instincts to get the job done. It's teamwork at its finest, and it shows just how clever dogs really are.

Their ability to help people goes beyond physical

tasks. Therapy dogs and emotional support animals have shown how powerful a dog's presence can be. They help people feel calm, safe, and less alone, simply by being themselves. Imagine walking into a hospital room feeling nervous, and there's a dog sitting there, wagging its tail and looking up at you with kind eyes. That dog doesn't know your story or why you're there, but it knows how to make you feel better. That's the kind of magic dogs bring to the world.

Of course, their incredible sense of smell deserves a moment of awe. A dog's nose is a scientific marvel, capable of detecting scents in ways humans can't even begin to imagine. They can smell diseases like cancer, track lost hikers, and even help protect endangered animals. Their noses are helping scientists make breakthroughs that save lives—not just for humans, but for other animals and the planet as a whole. And the best part? Dogs don't do it for fame or rewards. They do it because they love to help.

But dogs aren't just helpers—they're also friends. Every wag of their tail, every goofy grin, and every playful bark reminds us to enjoy the little things. They show us that happiness doesn't have to be complicated. A game of fetch, a belly rub, or a sunny spot to nap in can be all you need. Dogs have a way of reminding us what's really important: love, laughter, and spending time with the people (and animals) who make us feel at home.

Their diversity is another reason to marvel at dogs. From tiny Chihuahuas to massive Great Danes, from fluffy Pomeranians to sleek Greyhounds, there's a dog for every personality and lifestyle. Each breed brings something unique to the table, yet all dogs share that same ability to connect with humans in a way no other animal can. Whether they're a working dog with a serious job or a family pet whose main task is to cuddle, every dog has something special to offer.

Dogs have also shown us what it means to adapt. As humans have changed the way we live—moving from farms to cities, relying on technology, and traveling more than ever—dogs have changed right alongside us. They've learned to live in apartments, ride on airplanes, and even adjust to our modern schedules. Their adaptability shows how much they want to be a part of our lives, no matter what.

What truly sets dogs apart is their ability to bring people together. Whether it's a community coming together to rescue strays, families bonding over a shared love for their pet, or strangers striking up a conversation at the dog park, dogs have a way of connecting us. They remind us that kindness, patience, and love are what matter most, and they inspire us to be better people.

Even as the world changes, one thing will always stay the same: the special bond between humans and dogs. It's a relationship built on trust, loyalty, and mutual care, and it's unlike anything else on Earth. Dogs don't just live alongside us—they enrich our lives in ways we never expected. And for everything they give us, they ask for so little in return. A bit of food, a warm place to sleep, and someone to love—that's all a dog really needs to be happy.

Every dog, whether they're a hardworking service animal, a playful puppy, or a senior companion enjoying their golden years, has the power to make a difference. They teach us about love, bravery, and joy in ways that words never could. And as we look toward the future, it's clear that our connection with dogs will only grow stronger. Whether they're helping scientists, comforting the sick, or simply wagging their tail when we walk through the door, dogs will always have a special place in our hearts.

RESOURCES

Websites are a treasure trove of information for dog lovers. Some sites are designed to teach kids about dogs in fun and interactive ways. Websites like AKC.org (from the American Kennel Club) offer sections just for young dog enthusiasts, where you can learn about different breeds, training tips, and even games to play with your pup. Another great site is ASPCA.org, which has resources on animal care and ways to get involved in helping dogs in need.

For those who want to connect with other dog lovers, there are online forums and communities where people share advice, photos, and stories about their dogs. Websites like Dogster.com or DogTime.com are perfect for finding new ideas or simply enjoying pictures of adorable dogs from around the world. These sites also feature articles on health, training, and fun activities you can try with your dog.

If you're passionate about helping dogs, many organizations have resources to guide you. The Humane Society (HumaneSociety.org) is a fantastic place to learn about adoption, fostering, and ways to support animal welfare. They often have events like adoption drives or fundraising walks where you can get involved and meet other dog lovers.

Another organization worth checking out is Best Friends Animal Society (BestFriends.org). They work to rescue dogs, reduce the number of animals in shelters, and promote kindness toward all pets. Their website includes information on volunteering, donating, and even visiting their sanctuary in Utah, which is home to hundreds of animals waiting for forever homes.

If you're interested in therapy or service dogs, organizations like Canine Companions (CCI.org) or Therapy Dogs International (TDI-Dog.org) are great places to learn more. They offer programs and training for dogs who help people, from guiding the visually impaired to providing comfort in hospitals and schools. Reading about these programs can inspire you to think about how dogs and humans can work together to make the world a better place.

Libraries and local animal shelters are also excellent resources. Libraries often have sections devoted to pets, with books, magazines, and DVDs that can teach you about everything from caring for a dog to understanding their behavior. Many libraries even host events like storytimes with therapy dogs or workshops on pet care.

Shelters are more than just places where dogs wait for new homes—they're hubs of information and community support. Many shelters offer classes on dog training or behavior, and some even have kids' programs where you can volunteer or learn about how to care for animals. Visiting a shelter is a great way to see firsthand how people are working to help dogs in need.

If you love exploring with technology, apps about dogs can be fun and useful. There are apps for training, tracking your dog's health, and even identifying dog breeds. Apps like "BringFido" help you find dog-friendly parks, restaurants, and hotels, making it easier to include your dog in family outings. Others, like "Pupford," offer tips and videos on training, helping you build a stronger bond with your dog.

For kids who love projects, creating something to

help dogs is a great way to combine learning with action. You could design a poster to raise awareness about adoption, make toys or blankets for a local shelter, or start a blog to share your favorite dog facts and stories. These kinds of projects let you use your creativity to make a real difference.

GLOSSARY

Breed

A breed is a group of dogs that share similar characteristics, like size, fur type, and behavior. For example, Golden Retrievers are known for their friendly nature and golden fur, while Dachshunds are small with long bodies and short legs. Breeds are like dog "families," and each one has its own special traits.

Puppy

A puppy is a young dog, kind of like a baby in the dog world. Puppies are playful, curious, and need lots of care and training to grow into happy adult dogs. They also have sharp little teeth, which they use to explore everything—sometimes even things they shouldn't!

Muzzle

The muzzle is the part of a dog's face that includes their nose and mouth. It's what helps them sniff, breathe, and eat. Some dogs have long muzzles, like Greyhounds, while others have short muzzles, like Pugs. A muzzle can also refer to a safety device placed over a dog's mouth to prevent biting or chewing.

Paw

A paw is a dog's foot, which has pads on the bottom to help them walk, run, and grip surfaces. Dogs use their paws for lots of things, from digging to shaking hands. Each paw usually has four toes and a claw on each toe, plus a fifth claw called a dewclaw, which is like a thumb.

Tail Wagging

When a dog wags their tail, they're using it to communicate. Tail wagging doesn't always mean a dog is happy—it can also show excitement, nervousness, or curiosity. Watching how a dog wags their tail can give you clues about what they're feeling.

Fur

A dog's fur, also called a coat, covers their body and helps keep them warm or cool. Some dogs have short fur, while others have long, fluffy fur. There are even dogs with curly coats, like Poodles. Regular grooming keeps a dog's fur healthy and shiny.

Barking

Barking is a dog's way of talking. They bark to warn of danger, greet someone, or even ask for attention. Different barks can mean different things. A loud, sharp bark might say, "Stay away!" while a softer bark could mean, "Let's play!"

Growling

Growling is a low, rumbling sound that dogs make when they're upset or uncomfortable. It's their way of saying, "I don't like this." Growling doesn't always mean a dog is aggressive—it's how they warn others to back off or stop what they're doing.

Sniffing

Sniffing is how dogs explore the world. Their noses are super powerful, with about 300 million scent receptors (we humans only have 5 million). Sniffing helps them gather information, like who's been nearby or where food might be hiding.

Fetch

Fetch is a game where you throw something, like a ball or a stick, and the dog runs to get it and bring it back to you. Many dogs love this game because it taps into their natural instincts to chase and retrieve objects.

Collar

A collar is a band that goes around a dog's neck. It usually holds their ID tags, which include their name and the owner's contact information. Collars can also be used to attach a leash for walks.

Leash

A leash is a strap that connects to a dog's collar or harness, allowing their owner to guide them on walks. Leashes keep dogs safe by preventing them from running into traffic or getting lost.

Harness

A harness is an alternative to a collar. It fits around a dog's chest and shoulders, spreading out pressure if they pull on the leash. Some dogs, like small breeds or those with delicate necks, do better with a harness than a collar.

Sit

"Sit" is one of the first commands most dogs learn. It means the dog lowers their bottom to the ground and stays in place. This command helps dogs focus and behave in situations where they might otherwise jump or run around.

Stay

"Stay" tells a dog to remain in one spot until they're told otherwise. It's a useful command for keeping a dog safe or calm, especially in busy or distracting environments.

Heel

"Heel" is a command that asks a dog to walk close to their owner's side without pulling on the leash. It's helpful for walks in crowded places or during training sessions.

Crate

A crate is a small, enclosed space where a dog can rest or stay when their owner isn't home. Many dogs see their crate as a safe, cozy den. Crate training can help with housebreaking and give dogs a place to relax.

Housebreaking

Housebreaking, or potty training, is teaching a dog to go to the bathroom outside or in a designated spot. Puppies need time and patience to learn this skill, but once they do, it makes living together much easier.

Agility

Agility is a sport where dogs navigate a course with obstacles like tunnels, jumps, and weave poles. It's fast-paced and fun, showing off a dog's speed and focus. Agility training builds trust between dogs and their handlers.

Therapy Dog

A therapy dog is trained to comfort and support people in places like hospitals, schools, or nursing homes. These dogs aren't service animals, but they play an important role in helping people feel better.

Service Dog

A service dog is specially trained to help a person with a disability, like guiding someone who is blind or alerting someone to an oncoming seizure. These dogs are highly skilled and provide independence and safety for their owners.

Breed Rescue

A breed rescue is a group that helps find homes for specific breeds of dogs. If someone loves a certain breed but wants to adopt instead of buying, these rescues are a great option.

Spaying and Neutering

Spaying (for female dogs) and neutering (for male dogs) are surgeries that prevent dogs from having puppies. These procedures help control the dog population and can also reduce certain health risks.

Obedience Training

Obedience training teaches dogs how to follow commands and behave well. It's like school for dogs, helping them learn skills that make them great companions.

Separation Anxiety

Some dogs feel nervous or upset when they're left alone. This is called separation anxiety. Dogs with this condition might bark, chew, or pace when their owner leaves, but training and patience can help them feel more secure.

Dog Park

A dog park is a special area where dogs can run

and play off-leash. It's a great place for dogs to socialize and burn off energy while their owners chat with other dog lovers.

Microchip

A microchip is a tiny device implanted under a dog's skin. It holds an ID number that helps reunite lost dogs with their owners. A vet or shelter can scan the chip to access the owner's contact information.

Each of these terms opens a door to understanding dogs better. Whether it's learning how they communicate, exploring their incredible abilities, or simply getting to know the tools and commands that keep them happy, these words help us connect with our canine companions on a deeper level. The more you understand these terms, the more you can appreciate just how amazing dogs truly are.